E A R N I E
L A R S E N

His Last Steps

EARNIE and PAULA LARSEN

Foreword by Claudia Black, Ph.D.

HAZELDEN®

Hazelden
Center City, Minnesota 55012
hazelden.org

Library of Congress Cataloging-in-Publication Data

Larsen, Earnest.
   Earnie Larsen : his last steps / Earnie and Paula Larsen ; foreword by Claudia Black.
      p. cm.
    ISBN 978-1-61649-202-1 (softcover)
    ISBN 978-1-61649-427-8 (ebook)
1. Larsen, Earnest—Correspondence. 2. Larsen, Earnest—Diaries.
3. Larsen, Earnest—Health. 4. Conduct of life. 5. Twelve-step programs—Religious aspects—Christianity. 6. Self-help techniques—United States.
7. Recovery movement—United States. 8. Cancer—Patients—United States—Biography. 9. Counselors—United States—Biography.
10. Religious educators—United States—Biography.
I. Larsen, Paula Bendry. II. Title.
    HV28.L335A3 2012
    362.19699'4370092—dc23

                                                    2012006331

Editor's note

This publication is not intended as a substitute for the advice of health care professionals.

Alcoholics Anonymous and AA are registered trademarks of Alcoholics Anonymous World Services, Inc.

Earnie's letters have been edited slightly for grammar, punctuation, style, and clarity. The substance of his message remains the same.

Some names may have been changed to protect the privacy of those mentioned in this publication.

14 13 12   1 2 3 4 5 6

Cover design by David Spohn
Interior design and typesetting by Kinne Design

To

Erin and Monte,

Cara and John,

Montgomery, Loren, Josh,

Ella, Adeline, and Isabel

And, of course, "his guys"

contents

contents

PART TWO: LESSONS

foreword

Earnie and I spoke for the last time just four days prior to his passing. He told me that he was tired, but at the same time very much looking forward to speaking at Second Sunday, an annual ritual for him at the Hazelden Center, just a couple of days away. He couldn't have been filled with more love and joy as he told me about also taking along some of "his guys" from the local Salvation Army and Union Gospel Mission to share their stories. As you will read in *Earnie Larsen: His Last Steps,* it was only a day after this event that he was admitted to a hospital, where he died within the night. In our conversation, he spoke frankly of the seriousness of his condition and his regret that with his latest prognosis he had less time with his family than originally expected. He quickly went on to tell me how much he loved "his guys" and so hoped I would be able to meet them some day. He spoke of their pain, their fears, and their history, yet what he saw was their preciousness and value. He wanted them to feel those qualities for themselves. That conversation epitomized my experience of Earnie. He exuded love and compassion for all and was probably most comfortable with those who were the most broken. He knew they couldn't love themselves if they didn't have that love reflected back.

Earnie and I met professionally in the mid-1980s, often speaking at the same recovery conferences. As I would listen to him speak and tell stories of those he encountered, what I remember most was the passion and love he conveyed, the humor he could find in his own fallibilities, and the clarity he had about what was needed for change that would offer people the life they deserved—a life of love and connectedness with self, others, and the person's Higher Power. The two of us would often sit together in the back of the conference room listening to the next speaker. We didn't talk much, as we felt connected in heart to a mutual mission in our lives. We felt blessed that our personal mission was carried over into our professional lives. Both Earnie and I came from childhood histories that would shape who we were and undoubtedly the paths we would follow and pursue. In his presence I knew I was safe on all levels; I knew I was loved. For those of you who had any direct experience with Earnie, you understand what I mean. Being in his presence meant being ensconced in love and acceptance.

Earnie was a man with respect for all, a man without judgment. Oh, he could get angry and frustrated, but what frustrated him most was the lack of respect and compassion that people had for others and for the circumstances others had to endure. All the while he was a man of action truly living the Serenity Prayer.

> God, grant me the serenity
> to accept the things I cannot change,
> courage to change the things I can,
> and wisdom to know the difference.

Earnie had a wonderful manner of using metaphors and analogies. He was recognized for being a great listener, and his metaphors or analogies often came from people he'd met, from the person he sat next to on a park bench to the client in therapy at a psych ward. He challenged us to ask ourselves, "Who is driving our own bus?" Is it guilt, is it procrastination, our junkie self, our alcoholic or drug-dependent parent's rages? Our job is to ask the question and take responsibility for how we want to live our lives. Confronted with his own recovery, Earnie realized how difficult change was. He was full of compassion about the struggle, and as he said, "New behavior has to swim upstream despite entrenched feelings." But he also knew the possibilities when we quit "making changes" and committed to "change." He believed those possibilities occur when we allow ourselves to be in the presence of those who will love us when we can't do it for ourselves.

Earnie leaves us with many lessons, but his primary legacy is in his teachings about Stage II recovery in the addiction and recovery field. In his straightforward and often simple manner, he defined Stage II as "rebuilding of life after Stage I." At that time in our evolution, the notion that abstinence did not by itself define recovery was revolutionary. As Earnie said, "Getting out of a bad place didn't necessarily take you to a good place." Abstinence, he said, was like standing at the starting line. The race has not started, but at least you are standing, not lying down. Stage II recovery involves making the most of a life that has been rescued from obsession and addiction. Earnie believed that learning to make relationships work was at the core of full recovery, and he would go on to recognize that it was the lack of skills that so often interfered. This incredibly caring, dynamic man, often wearing his trademark suspenders, would challenge all of us to leave our comfort zones and look at our self-defeating behaviors. Earnie talked about the essence of recovery being "the ability to hear the flutter of angel wings as all around us are countless quiet moments of spiritual growth unfolding." Let us honor Earnie in his teachings by listening to the flutter.

Earnie had a strong faith in his God and was steeped in Twelve Step principles. He lived his spirituality in daily practice. In *Earnie Larsen: His Last Steps,* you will read how God pointed him toward the burning houses that His children were in—the children who didn't know their worthiness; didn't know they could be forgiven; didn't know how special and beautiful they were. Earnie was directed toward these individuals and believed his God was with him "every step of the way."

He always valued strength, always honored the tough people he came to know. That is why he loved "his guys" so much. They survived the streets. He believed there was nothing to fear when surrounded by unconquerable strength, with the greatest strength being love. He would say, "I did my best to not drop any of you." I truly hope he knows that we believe him.

In this book he offers lessons about dying. He recognized cancer was a part of his journey, part of the bigger picture. He would say, "Cancer can't hurt me, at least not the part of me that is more than my body. And that is most of me." For Earnie, it was "a new chapter that would hold wonderful things hiding there in the dark." He was anxious to grab hold of every one of them.

Although Earnie was frustrated he didn't have more time on this earth, he was grateful to live beyond the years of most men who preceded him in his family, feeling he had dodged the bullet. He was surprised when he became sick. If he was angry at all, it was because he didn't have more time. He was told during his illness that he didn't need to run into the burning houses anymore; yet, as he said, "Nothing else seemed more important to do or that I would rather do."

He had learned a lesson earlier in life: When one is tired, one just needs to take "ten more steps." In his final passage, Earnie came to understand he didn't have to take even one more step, and he embraced the beauty that came with this acceptance. As he said, "I just need to stop and let the grace that surrounds me fill me up."

In *Earnie Larsen: His Last Steps,* Earnie and his courageous wife, Paula, take us into their lives, sharing with us one of the most profound and intimate life experiences. It has been an honor to share a part of their journey. Earnie could not respond to the many people who reached out to him in his final months, but he asked that we go to the essence of that place where our spirits cross and know that he is there for us. To Adeline and Montgomery, we will keep talking about your grandfather—our friend—and he will be forever in our hearts. And to Loren, who could hear his grandpa cheering for him all across town, I believe if we listen, we can hear him cheering for all of us as well.

Claudia Black, Ph.D.

preface

Earnie has always been a writer, so it wasn't a surprise when he began writing letters soon after he was diagnosed with pancreatic cancer. Earnie and I talked over each round/letter and lesson, and then we sent them out. At first, we sent them to family members to keep them updated on Earnie's condition. It wasn't long, however, before the list of recipients expanded to include friends—and then friends of friends. Many people contacted us about how deeply touched they felt after reading the letters. Many of them also suggested the letters be compiled into a book to serve as a guide for those walking this road, or for those seeking what they are called to do in this life. We both thought that was a good idea, but that is where it ended. Back then, we thought we had plenty of time to get to this book—at least two years. But the time he had left ended up being much shorter than we had predicted, and the project was left unfinished.

After his funeral, people still said, "I sure hope you do something special with these letters and lessons. They could help so many people." Now that Earnie was gone, I wasn't sure this was possible. But then I thought about how he wrote his other books: Earnie wrote the rough draft, and I polished it off and sent it out. In the end, this book wasn't any different from his others. I deeply felt his presence as I wrote my part of the book.

This is really a book of letters; it is broken up into what Earnie called "rounds," which refer to "a course of prescribed duties, actions, etc." (*Webster's New College Dictionary*) and "lessons." After each of Earnie's letters, I offer my reflections or comments on the time or the idea. This is not a book to hurry through, even though you may want to do that. I recommend reading one letter at a time and then letting it digest. Read one per day or per week and find another person to share and talk about your thoughts and feelings. As our Program says, "Take what you like and leave the rest."

Peace and love,
Paula

acknowledgmentf

I wish to acknowledge the valuable assistance of the Hazelden Foundation and Nick Motu, publisher, for accepting and trusting me to deliver this manuscript even though Earnie had passed. Thanks also to Hazelden's executive editorial director, Sid Farrar, who said, "This will be a labor of love," and to my sister, Ellen, who helped me edit the pages, but more importantly, encouraged me through each page. This felt like a long process but one I very much wanted to do. Finally, I'd like to thank Jody Klescewski from Hazelden for all her help and support, and April Ebb.

PART ONE

Rounds

Let People Love You

October 4, 2010

Dear family/friends/loved ones/team,

You are all of those, and more.

I want to fill you in on how I am and what is happening with me. Actually, it is pretty cool in some ways.

All my life people have told me—well, at least for the past forty-plus years—"You've got to let people love you. You need to learn to receive. You need to just stand still and be one with God."

Of course it made sense. I know and knew that loving someone but not being able to accept his or her love in return was like driving on half a wheel. Loving is good, but it is not better than allowing myself to be loved. Both are critical for the wheel to be whole. Johnny McAndrew and I made a whole CD called *The Promise* on just that point.

I didn't really know how to do the "let yourself be loved" part. What I did know was, when God sent someone across my path who felt "less than, unloved, unimportant," it was my job to jump in and go get them. When God said, "Let's go," I knew how to say, "Okay, just show me where you want me to go."

As a result, I've had a front-row seat at some of the most amazing miracles imaginable. I would have hated to miss even one of them. I saw the power of love (which to me is the power of God) do the impossible. I've seen the dead man Lazarus come out of the tomb full of life and grace a million times. But somewhere along the line I missed the understanding that I, too, am Lazarus. And my God would heal me as soon as He healed those He sent across my path.

The first few days after I got the cancer card, I couldn't believe it; it seemed totally unreal. I didn't get knocked off my square so much as knocked down on my square. Everything was heavy, dark, and depressing.

Then last Tuesday—in that creepy, amazing way spiritual things always seem to happen—my inner voice spoke to me. It told me to get up, reach out, make contact, and stay not just connected but super-connected. So I decided to go over to the Sally (Salvation Army Adult Rehabilitation Center) and see my guys for lunch. I wanted them to see that I didn't look like some Halloween monster on his last legs. We had a wonderful time! So much love and concern. So much power!

There has been so much love from all the emails, calls, cards, and even flowers. Each was and is like some kind of spiritual doorbell ringing and saying, "Open up. Let us in. We are here for you." Each morning, Paula hands me the newest batch of emails to read. They are like looking outside and seeing sunshine and flowers.

I had also called my pastor, Johnny Hunter, and asked if Paula and I could drop over for the Tuesday night Bible study/prayer group and get some really good laying on of hands. Being there felt like sitting in the middle of a huge whirlpool—all that faith, love, and community pouring in and over me (and Paula as well) in abundant measure.

What I came away with was an overwhelming sense that no matter what happens, I am and will be okay. And so will everyone else. Somehow on that deep level where things really matter, I had a sense that the Father had scooped me up, like in the famous poem "Footprints in the Sand," and if I was in my Father's arms, outcomes didn't matter. I was safe and would be fine no matter what happened. And when our "okayness" doesn't depend on specific outcomes, but rather on who is holding us, we are safe beyond any power that could destroy us.

After the prayer service, I was talking to Sid, Newsome, and Ernie outside. I asked them if Jonathon had gotten into treatment. Had anyone seen Wardell? Had Bobby surfaced since getting out of prison? They all told me to stop worrying about them. They said they would take care of the guys in the wind (out in the cold/on the streets). What I needed to do was focus on myself and take care of me. It's true. And I am in a place where that lesson is actually sinking in.

Yes, I'm listening to the doctors. Yes, I am doing everything they say. Yes, I am doing everything I know how to do to move through this cancer thing as best I can. But I want you all to know there is also something far more powerful at play in me. Whatever happens, I'll be okay. And so will you.

I'm fine. I feel good. I don't look like a Halloween monster on its last legs. I may very well have many years of life on earth left. I hope so. But the important (and new) element is that I am okay no matter what happens. And so are you. Father has us all in His loving arms. If Father has us, nothing can harm us—no matter what happens.

Love to you all. (I'm thinking of entering a seniors boxing tournament next month.)

Earnie

———

...nesday, September 29, his doctor called to tell us that ...e wanted to hospitalize Earnie so that Earnie could receive a couple of pints of blood. His hemoglobin was down to 6.7, when it should have been in the teens. September 29 was our thirty-first anniversary, but instead of doing something fun that day, we went to the hospital. We waited and waited for the blood, or so it seemed. At about 5:00 p.m., they gave him blood and then began the prep for the tests scheduled for the next day. On Friday afternoon, his doctor who was assigned to him at the hospital called me out into the hall to show me the results of Earnie's tests: He had found pancreatic cancer. He decided a specialist should explain everything and answer our questions, which is why he didn't tell us the news in Earnie's room. When I went back into the room, I decided to tell Earnie the news myself, since secrets aren't good.

We had some time before the specialist came in to mull over what the doctor had told me. We thought they would probably do chemo first and then surgery. You know the saying "Life changes on a dime"? Well, that was true for us. No cancer, and then—*cancer*! Everything changes right then and there. The world keeps turning, when it feels like it should stop!

So we went home that night. The next day I went off to my Saturday morning women's support group, where

I asked for prayers and shared what the doctors thought they had found.

And to say God has a sense of humor is no small thing. Saturday afternoon, as I was putting some meat on our grill, I saw Earnie's car shake and then heard a loud crash. It turned out that a teenage driver with only a permit had come whipping around our corner and went right up into our driveway, hitting Earnie's car and breaking our garage door in half. This also pushed my car, which was inside the garage, into the wall of our packing room, where we kept Earnie's DVD inventory. The young driver panicked and tried to back up, hitting Earnie's car again. As one of our friends later said, "It looked like someone was on a bender." But she wasn't drinking or using; it was just inexperience.

Well, that was a major distraction, and I have come to believe that often God will give me/us too much to handle so that I/we will ask for His help. And believe me, we needed it here. No cars working, the garage door split in two, and the walls of the packing room smashed. What's more, Earnie was scheduled at a different medical facility for a special test in a couple of days. But God is good, and doors and walls are only things. And thankfully, no one was hurt. Our daughter Cara had been in the driveway just twenty minutes before all of this happened. Her car was right where all the action took place! But she was unharmed. God is good! Soon after this incident, the prayer shawls began arriving, and boy did we need them! The beige one was made by some women in recovery and brought by my "Sacred Sister" Virginia and her husband Steve.

A few days later, Earnie's special test was done, and it confirmed the cancer diagnosis. We made an appointment with the oncologist. Earnie's internist, Dr. Jerry Noller, had called with the names of two oncologists even before Earnie had the test, and my comment was, "Isn't this a little early?" But right after the test, we needed to choose an oncologist, and I had the names, thanks to his doctor.

The oncology appointment was scheduled immediately. In our minds, we were still thinking chemo and then surgery. But, in the meantime, I contacted a friend at the Mayo Clinic to ask for his input and to check on the possibility of a second opinion. I am from Rochester, so the Mayo Clinic is what I think of first. My friend very wisely said to wait until we met with the oncologist to see what he had to say; we could always get a second opinion later. Our prayers were that it would become clear to us what the next action should be. And at the time Earnie was wondering, *Why do chemo?*

Our daughter Cara came with us for the appointment with the oncologist. It was so helpful to have her with us;

for anyone in a similar situation, I highly recommend taking another family member along to hear what is being said and to provide support.

. . .

Round 2

No Secrets

October 6, 2010

Dear family/friends/loved ones/team,

Families don't keep secrets, so here is what's going on:

My cancer is Stage IV, which means neither surgery nor radiation is possible. The oncologist said there are some types of chemo that I could try, but the side effects seemed second only to the crucifixion! What was to be gained by the chemo seemed insignificant. Although no one (on earth) knows how long I have, the doctor said it wasn't unreasonable to expect two years even if I "did nothing."

Actually, I found this rather good news. From the start, I had pretty much decided I didn't want the side effects of putting a bunch of poison in my system, especially since I am feeling—in some ways—better than I ever have. So, to hell with the poison. I'll "do nothing" for eight weeks or so and then go back and get another CT scan to "check the markers" and see where I (meaning Paula and I) want to go from there.

So, that's that. Now let me tell you about the ways my life has never been better:

I was telling my brother Bill that I was feeling a bit guilty staying in bed longer than I ever would before. He opened a beautiful door for me (thanks, Bill) by asking why I didn't see the bed as the loving arms of God and all the people who love me. While I always would have thought that was a lovely sentiment, in the past I would have let it bounce off me like a Ping-Pong ball off a cement wall. But not now. This morning I was able to stay in bed till almost 10, *and loved it*! I've never been able to do that before. It's really quite cool.

Someone else told me, "You don't have to run into any more burning houses to save people." Maybe so, or at least not in the same way. But I want everyone to know that I loved running into those burning houses. There is nothing else that seemed more important to do or that I would rather do.

For over fifty years, I've had this covenant with God. He pointed me to the burning house and told me that His children were in there and He wasn't going to lose them. He told me clear as a whistle in my ear, "They don't know they are worth anything. They don't know they can be forgiven. They don't know I love them no matter what. They don't know how special and beautiful they are. So you go show them. I'll be with you every step of the way. So let's get up and get going."

Nothing was better or more important than playing a part in creating the tipping point where people blasted out of their prisons and came walking out of their tombs with faces shining like the sun.

But now it is like I've been transferred to a new department. I have new glasses. My job now is to "stay in bed and feel the arms of a loving God and all those who send me their love." I still have stacks of letters and emails to get out. I still have projects to do and books to write piled up on my desk, etc. I guess they are part of the burning house too. Some I may do or not do—but it's no longer a matter of life or death. What does matter now is being still and delving deeper into the mystery that God is good (all the time), and that with God, if we let ourselves be held, everything will be okay.

Now, about "doing nothing" about the cancer for the next two years. I don't plan on doing nothing and I hope you don't, either. Man proposes; God disposes. Two years is a long time. And the God we know cares nothing for human time frames. I'll go home (as we all will) when God is good and ready. Two minutes, two weeks, two years, twenty years—who knows? Paula and I will do everything we can to stay strong, stay up, stay in faith and prayer. I think it would be a fine joke on the medical establishment to go maybe twenty years or beyond. So we ask you to continue in prayer with us that God's will be done. I'm fine and so are you.

Onward in peace and faith,
Earnie

———

{PAULA} Dr. King, his oncologist, said it was Stage IV pancreatic cancer and that neither surgery nor radiation would be helpful. He then told us about the possibility of chemo, but added it would only prolong Earnie's life for an additional *six weeks or so*! That message was loud and clear. Dr. King said around 5 percent of the people with this cancer live about two years, and I immediately put Earnie into that category, as did Earnie and our daughter Cara. Before the diagnosis, I thought we would have about twenty more years together, especially after he turned seventy. That was longer than his father or any of the other male Larsens had lived, although shorter than his mother's lifespan. But it was not to be. Still, two years didn't sound so bad, since a lot can happen in two years.

The chemo person came in but we told her of our decision, so that was a short visit. The nutritionist came in and gave us some good help and insights. She answered our questions and gave us a list of good, easily digestible foods for Earnie; little did we know then what a big part diet would play in the months ahead.

It was not the message we wanted, but it is what we got, and so we said, "We go on from here." We still thought we had about two years. Although I still wanted twenty more with him, two was good, and maybe in those two years they would find a cure.

. . .

Round 3

Come with Me on My Journey

October 11, 2010

Dear family/friends/team/loved ones,

I had an idea the other day. It might have even been a good idea. You'll have to let me know.

Ever since high school, I have found writing to be a good friend. It has allowed me to clarify my thoughts and feelings, blow off steam, and pay attention to my own and others' lives. So it's no surprise I find myself writing during this new chapter in my life. Some of that writing has been in the form of the two letters I recently sent to you.

I also write in what I call a God File; have for years. It's just a record of what I have seen and learned as I try to pay attention. There must be close to a thousand pages in the file. Mostly no one sees that writing, not that there are any secrets there. It's just that we've never made a link (or know how to) so anyone could see it—if anyone wanted to.

Many of you have responded that you enjoyed (or whatever the right word is) the two letters. As I say, I'm going to be writing my reports on what's going on with me during this time, no matter what.

The "idea" I mentioned earlier was that some of you might be interested in coming with me through these letters on this leg of my journey. Maybe it's all just my crazy ego to think anyone would be interested, but I know I don't want to go down this road more alone than necessary. No secrets. As my KCA sponsor tells me, if you don't tell people you want them to go with you, how would they know? (KCA stands for Kicking Cancer's Ass.)

Onward,
Earnie

———

{PAULA} I started sending off Earnie's letters in emails to our family first, then started to include friends. The response was overwhelming. Earnie was most touched. He then decided he would keep on doing the letters. Dying is life's biggest secret—and when the dying person lets you walk with him or her, that is indeed a gift. I had received this gift many years back from my friend Nell. My journey with her helped me with this journey. A lesson for me:

If we process and learn from one thing, that helps prepare us for the next thing. So I started emailing Earnie's letters to many friends.

. . .

Round 4

You Blow Me Over

October 13, 2010

Dear family/friends/team/loved ones,

I'm knocked over by all the emails—both from inside and outside the country. I love them all. But they do present a problem . . .

Some of you who sent emails I don't know at all. Some I don't really know, but you know me through various talks, books, etc. (And I am deeply grateful that you found something helpful in that connection.) But many of you I do indeed know. And more than know—we have touched on that level where life holds its deepest meaning. We have left a piece of ourselves in that sacred place. You know who you are. You know our story. We marched out and did battle with the beast of fear and all the lies that would chain us to the rock of "I'm not worthy." To all those lies, we leaned on each other and shouted, "Yes I am! I am the best me that ever was!" We made war on the darkness and so entered the light.

Oh my, there are so many battles! So many worthwhile, necessary, and heroic, wonderful battles fought. Again, you know who you are. I hesitate to say even a single name. Because behind that name are hundreds and hundreds of other names equally beautiful and important in my sight. All such precious faces, precious people fighting the good fight and reaching up to God like giant sunflowers on a bright day. You have often made me feel ten feet tall and bulletproof.

You never forget people you have been to war with. And that's my problem—I'd love to send each of you a super-duper response. I sit here with a stack of over two hundred emails, wishing I had the strength to go back with you to that sacred place where we first met, look around, and know, "We did good here, didn't we?" Just think how improbable our meetings were. Every one of you shouting, "God is good—all the time." God's fingerprints are all over us.

But I can't respond to each of you. So I ask you, again knowing who you are, to go in spirit to that place where our spirits crossed and know that I am there for you, in you, and with you, just as you are for me.

God has almost always used—and does use—others to make His presence known among us. In the Old Testament, it was Abraham, Moses, and the prophets. In the New Testament, He even sent Jesus to take a form just like ours so we could best understand The Word. He came in our form to tell us that God is Father and that we are never beyond His reach. And so it is with you and your emails. I so clearly hear the Voice behind all your voices—I see and feel the Love behind all the love you send me. I feel His Presence as you gather around me. The Father is so powerfully present and made manifest through you.

Also—not that I quite know the right words for this—life hurts everyone. We've all lost parts of our heart and soul. We've all been deeply hurt. Some of us from our earliest years. Everyone has been sliced deep. In response to those hurts, we find all kinds of tricky ways to hide and protect ourselves. Those ways work, more or less. At some point, they may have even saved our lives. But they also become barriers to accessing precisely what we most seek.

Well, I'm here to tell you as the Presence and Love of the Father becomes more apparent—like a laser light focusing on a specific point—it is exactly at that point where we most hurt, seek, fear, and hope that our Father comes to heal and fulfill. That first! There first! He comes as the gentlest Healer seeking our deepest hurt—and there His grace abounds. Nothing of this earth is stronger than or can stand against Father coming for His children. The more deeply hurt, the more Father hurries to rescue us, scoop us up, and say "Welcome" into the deepest part of our spirits.

I ask, "Where have you been all these years?" And Father responds, "I've been right here, waiting for you to be ready to be healed." In this way, I've come to clearly understand that whatever we have lost shall be returned to us a thousand fold. I found that to be very, very good news.

This feels very important to me. Those of you who have expressed to me your fears and staggering losses and doubt and hesitancy to surrender into the arms of our all-loving God: It is YOU I hold up. Father comes to you as fast as we will allow. He's good. Allowing ourselves to be scooped up and held and loved and healed is really good! I am sitting in Father's lap right now. He told me to tell you this. He wants you to know you are a *champion*!

As I said, I don't know all the right words to speak to your hearts, but I do know this: God is faithful. He knows our deepest hopes and fears. He knows our names. He knows where we are hurt and at some point He takes over and says to each of us, "Okay, you did your best. Now let me do for you what you could never do for yourself." It's all very cool to watch.

Many of you sent me your suggestions and offers of

remedies. Most seem to have to do with boosting my immune system and detoxifying the poisons in my body. We could make a book of all the suggestions. (Maybe we should?) Be assured that I am on a power-packed program from both those angles. We are doing every earthly thing we can to be as healthy as we (Paula and I) can for as long as we can.

But also know this: I'm not dead yet, and, if it pleases the Father, I won't be for quite some time. I feel good. I told my fifteen-year-old grandson, Josh, that I ran a four-minute mile yesterday. He said, "Well you can't be all that sick if you're still saying such weird things."

Many of you mentioned fear in one way or another. I have not the least speck of fear. Cancer can't hurt me, at least not that part of me that is more than my body. And that is most of me. So what is there to be afraid of?

My overriding emotion at this time is—and probably is a good sign of how far I have to go in my recovery!—bring it on! Let's see where this all goes. I feel like Howard Carter, who discovered King Tut's burial tomb in 1922. When his team finally broke a hole in the wall to his chamber, Carter stuck his head in the hole and shined his flashlight around. Someone said, "What do you see?" He said, "Wonderful things," as his light glanced off all the gold in the room.

Certainly not everything about cancer is "wonderful," but it is part of a journey. It's part of a bigger picture. It's a new chapter that has many "wonderful things" hiding there in the dark. And I am anxious to grab hold of every one of them.

I've always valued strength. I was raised to seek and honor and cleave to strength wherever I found it. I've always honored the "tough people" I've known. Maybe that's part of why I love "my guys" so much. They survived the streets. They fight way above their weight class. What is there to fear if we are surrounded by unconquerable strength?

I've learned the greatest strength is love. And I've learned the source of all love is my Father. My Father has pulled me close. I am surrounded by abundant love. Cancer has no hold on me that matters. So bring it on. Let's see where it all goes.

So anyway, know that I love you all. The Father is amply, abundantly manifested in your love to me. I thank you for that. If you need to talk, go to that place where we went to war against fear and lies. I'll meet you there with Father —we'll have a picnic.

Onward,
Earnie

———

{PAULA} Every morning I would come down to my office (Earnie's office and mine are right across from each other), boot up my computer, then print off and read the numerous emails before I started my work. They were so very touching and personal. We often talked about how open people felt they could be in their emails to Earnie—permission was given to share what they had wanted to share with him for years, but up until now they hadn't. God is good!

On Thursday, October 14, we went over to Stillwater, which, for those of you who don't live in Minnesota, is on the St. Croix River and a breathtakingly lovely city. Our fall weather was good, and so were the views. We had lunch overlooking the river, and it was great. About three hours after we got home, I got sick— and wow, was I sick. I asked Earnie if he could go out and get me some Gatorade. I was desperate and had terrible stomach cramps. As I was thinking about all of this, I started to laugh and said, "Don't we make a fine pair. What a team." We have been a team for thirty-one years.

· · ·

Round 5

Never Give Up or Give In

October 18, 2010

My dear companions on this journey,

No matter what, we must never give up or give in. Whatever comes at us in life, we have access to all the Power we need to not be defeated by it.

Tonight I have a headache and a few other aches and pains. I feel like I am stuck in a swamp of tar. My doc said that with my compromised immune system, I'd catch any illness people around me had. Paula had a touch of the flu the past few days. I caught it.

Isolation is always death. So I want to share with you a lovely, powerful moment that was given to me last Friday. It happened at the Sally (Salvation Army) during the class I teach.

I felt really good and wanted to be with my guys. The more I give them, the more they give me. So I showed up and did my class.

Having cancer seems to give me more credibility. I

equated my cancer with the addiction we all share. They are the same in that they both want to kill us. Recovery for both is the same in that without a total, 100 percent commitment to grab on to the God of our salvation, we don't stand a chance. I told them the story of "Mine."

Some of you know what that is. For those who don't, let me explain. Maybe ten years ago, Paula and I were in Ireland working at a treatment center called Hope House. Saturday morning was visiting time for families. I happened to be in the lobby as the families waited for their loved ones to come around the corner. Among those who waited were a young mother and her son of about five or six. When the dad came around the corner, the little boy took off like a shot. He wasn't playing around. No hesitation. No wondering if it was allowed or not. He was going hell-bent for election to his dad. He jumped into his dad's arms, grabbed him fiercely, and said with a passion that goes to the heart of what it means to be human, "Mine!" Both father and son had what their hearts most needed.

By telling this story, the point I was making to every man in this room of champions was that we need to "grab ahold of God" in the same way the little boy did. If we allow any space between us and God, the dogs of hell will come blasting through and eat our hearts.

Like I say, I was feeling good, so I took the next step. As I was telling the story, I noticed my dear friend Malik come in the back door and make his way to the outside seat in the front row. Malik works in the kitchen, so he is late sometimes getting to class. He's quite a guy. He has a ruggedly handsome face. He also has more muscles than a human body should be able to carry.

Anyway, I asked Malik to come up and stand by me. I again told the hundred or so men, "You got to grab ahold! You got to stop being timid. We are all fighting for our lives. You got to climb on and hang on for all you are worth."

Then I grabbed Malik as hard as I could. I grabbed him and growled, "Mine!" God is MINE, and I am never going to let go.

I've acted out the MINE point in a lot of places. I've always focused on how hard we must hang on to God. True enough. But the lovely gift I got this time was a new awareness that, yes, we need to hang on to Father—but what is equally true is that our Father is hanging on to us just as hard as we hang on to Him. I guess I had never thought of that before.

Malik caught on to our little show and hugged me back. I almost started laughing, thinking how he could hug me so hard my eyes would pop out if he wanted. He's one strong man. But he didn't. He hugged me enough to make the point; then, amazingly (at least to me), this great big man who knows all about the streets and gangs and prison laid his head on my shoulder. It felt like being lifted up by a thousand butterflies.

I knew Father was talking to me through Malik—He had a message for me. I didn't get a chance to listen to what that message was until I was driving home. It was quiet in the car. In my experience, God most often speaks to us in silence. Anyway, this is what I heard in my heart:

> Malik could have squeezed you to putty; so could I. But he didn't, and neither would I. Malik would never hurt you. Neither would I. I've never hurt you. I never caused you pain. I've never left you alone in the desert. There were times you didn't see me, but I never left you. There were a lot of times you were hurt and felt lost, but you never were. I always knew where you were. If one of us knows where you are, then you can't be lost. I have you, and I won't let go. Whatever rough water is ahead of you, don't worry about it. When it gets tough, I'll carry you. You have nothing to worry about. Relax—you have rushed into a million burning houses with me. So just breathe and know I am with you in your burning house.

At least it was something like that. Not so much specific words as a direct feed from Father's heart into mine. I knew what He meant and I am grateful—and free. Nothing is bigger than Father.

And this is exactly what I am going to tell the guys next Friday.

So thank you, Malik, and all of you wonderful companions who send me so much love. I accept it all.

Onward,
Earnie

———

{PAULA} On Friday nights we would have dinner together after he finished his class down at the Sally. It was always a special time with lots of sharing, many stories, and good food. When people are trying their best, what more can we ask?

One of the hardest parts for me since Earnie's passing is not having him home when I arrive, but more importantly, not being able to discuss what is going on in life. He wrote from home, so he was in the house more than I was. We talked over so many things. Now I find myself still talking with him, especially as I enter a room.

* * *

I was driving to the funeral of a friend's husband, and I could see the Basilica of St. Mary in the distance. I was thinking of all the people who were praying for a miracle for Earnie. I hoped they wouldn't be disappointed if he wasn't cured. It was then that I realized the miracle had already happened. We both felt very loved and supported by our God. That is by far the biggest gift—not necessarily to be healed, which both of us would certainly love and accept, but to know and believe that we are carried. What more can I really ask of this life? This doesn't mean that I won't face hard stuff; it means that I'm not alone—He walks with me.

At that funeral I saw my friend's mother, and she told me her sister had had pancreatic cancer and died within six months. A bell went off in my head, and I remember thinking, *We probably don't have two years. Our time is going to be shorter.* Yet I certainly didn't realize how short that time was to be.

· · ·

Round 6

Always Learning
an Important Lesson

October 20, 2010

Dear companions on the road,

I learned an important lesson today. I was fellowshipping with a bunch of my guys. We were having a good time laughing and saying outrageous things. Then out of the blue one of the brothers next to me got real serious, looked me in the eye, and said, "I'm scared."

Thinking it was all about me, I said, "Don't be scared for me. I'm doing fine. I'm going to be okay." He responded, "I'm not scared for you. I'm scared for me. When you are gone, who will ever love me like you have?"

That was my lesson. In relationships, there is no such thing as "just me." Relationships are about "us." In relationships, two is the smallest number. All this time since my diagnosis, I had only been thinking of me. I forgot about the *us*.

Lots of you might respond, "Don't worry about it. Your

job now is learning the lessons God is sending your way. Stop worrying about others. Leave the people in all the burning houses to others, at least for now."

I get that. I really do. But that is not the whole story. There is a covenant that goes with burning houses. Burning houses are all about paralyzing fear, horrendous guilt and shame, being trapped in a cave darker than night. It's about paralysis and rage and feeling so far down the throat of the beast there is no hope of ever seeing sunlight again.

If a person is willing to go into that mess, reach out a hand and invite the other to stand up, to lean on me, to start walking one baby step at a time out of that tomb— that is where the covenant is born. For if we ask that other person to trust us enough to get up and get going, and they do, the covenant—implicit or said in very clear, specific words—is "Swear you won't drop me. If I go with you, you *must* not drop me or I am sure I will die. If I let you love me, even a little, you must not betray me!"

I suppose this sounds overly dramatic to some, but not to others. Many of you know exactly what I mean. We've been there. We've faced the fear, shook the dust off our feet, and got the hell out of that dark place. We might have wobbled a good bit, but we trusted in the power of our Father, turned our face to the light, and got going.

Not all of you are addicts and felons. But fear and spiritual imprisonment are equal-opportunity bullies. They live in the cracks where the soul has been damaged. Countless is the number of the walking wounded with torn souls. I am not dead yet and may not be for a long time, but we have made a fine war on evil, haven't we? And for a long time, and all of it was God's business. All of it was for and from and to the Father.

I did my best to not drop any of you. I understood the covenant as well as you did. Where our paths crossed is *holy ground.* So, as this brother opened my eyes and told me of his fear, it became pretty obvious that my journey is about a whole lot more than just me. I knew that; I guess I just lost my focus. I offered you a hand (and a heart) in troubled times. If that hand lets go, whether of my choosing or not, of course it leaves a hole in your spirit. I am so sorry for that. I hate the thought of you, any of you, being in pain.

My only real thought on this is that "if God brought you to it, God will see you through it." The Father brought us together for a reason. His faithfulness never wavers. He holds me and you and all of us in the hollow of His hand. There is nothing that happens to us, or can happen to us, that is bigger than God. If we let the Father hold us, there is nothing to fear.

Lessons. Life is all about lessons, isn't it? I've only been figuring out what lessons there are for me in this cancer thing. I see now there are lessons for all of us as we go down this road together.

Onward,
Earnie

P.S. For some reason this thought just popped up: A good friend of mine from a long time ago, Father John Powell S.J., always signed his letters, "Remember me as loving you." Lovely, isn't it?

———

{PAULA} It was the middle of October, and he was down at the Sally with his guys. When he came home, we had a great talk and many, many tears together. He was very weepy, probably the most I had ever seen in all our years together. He was realizing what his departure would mean to so many—the guys, his friends, his grandchildren, his family. It was the question from one of the brothers at the Sally that spurred this understanding, that Earnie was leaving them and us. Up until this time, I don't think it had really dawned on him. We cried together about what the loss would be. For my part, I said, "I know I will be okay, but I will miss the hell out of you." As I said, I have always loved coming back to our house, greeting Earnie with a hug and a kiss and talking about our day. I will miss that the most. We had definitely fallen into a new, deeper level of love. From that day forward, much of his energy was spent trying to connect everyone.

Today was Grandparent's Day at Hill-Murray. Loren (a senior) and Josh (a freshman) met us first for Mass and then a lovely breakfast. It was a hard day for me, as I realized it might be the last day like this at school that we would spend together. Ever since the grandchildren were born, we visited them one day a week and had playtime with them. There is a short window of opportunity with grandchildren when you are so important in their lives and formation, and somehow we were blessed with the knowledge to take advantage of this time.

After eating and visiting at Hill-Murray, we always go to the Spirit shop to purchase sweatshirts to wear for the upcoming hockey season. I felt very strongly about once again buying both Earnie and me a new one for this season. As it turns out, I have worn both sweatshirts on numerous occasions other than hockey. It was a good thing to do! I take Earnie with me. It is what the ritual means that counts.

. . .

Round 7

God's Will

October 23, 2010

Dear companions on the journey,

Several people told me today in their emails that they were "mad at God" about my cancer. One said she was mad at fate. Another one said, "A wretched alignment of planets caused this tragedy."

One of those who was mad at God said, "What else can you call your diagnosis but God's will? Everything happens by His design. But why does God's will always have to be so brutal?"

If anger is a stage some people have to pass through to get to the other side, so be it. As I said in the previous letter, maybe this is a time for all of us to learn a few new lessons. Separation brings sadness. It would dishonor the love so many of us have found with each other to discount the sadness. But sadness is far from the whole picture! (As I constantly tell the guys at the Sally, "NDY!" —I'm not dead yet. My plan, if it is my Father's will, is that

I'll be around for a long time. So stop looking like someone stole your only pair of shoes.)

Let me tell you a bit of what I think of "God's will." At least God's will as I see it now.

I know for a fact, especially from my new perspective, that the Father loves us all. He loves us in a way made manifest in Jesus.

I know for a fact that love does not hurt the one loved.

I know for a fact my Father does nothing to hurt me. Never would. Never has. Never will.

I know for a fact my Father's will for me is only what is good for me and for my benefit.

Yes, everything I learned about God's will in school seemed to be anything other than what I wanted. The phrase "God's will" came to feel like having my house foreclosed. It was an unstoppable force that sought to take away whatever my rather deviant teenage soul wanted.

But that was then. Now is now. Now is new.

I look back over my life now and am aware of such huge blessings that were also God's will that I feel I need to shade my eyes from the glory. Far better than ten thousand Nobel Peace Prizes have been given to me by God's will. He has shown me His power and love all my life.

Sometimes I wasn't prepared to recognize the gifts as gifts. I dug my heels in, but God kept pouring on the grace.

We are what we see. We see what we are prepared to see. We become prepared through practice. And what I see and feel fills me with gratitude. I see God's fingerprints on every step of my past. Here are but two examples dear to my heart:

1. In the previous letter, I shared a moment of precious grace. It happened in the midst of messing around in fellowship with the guys. One of the men looked at me and said he was scared. He said he was afraid that after I passed (NDY, I told him) no one would love him the way I do.

We then had a good talk. He felt that through me came a thin shadow of his Father's love for him. That conversation went on for some time. But my point about God's will is this:

Love was as inaccessible to this man as a flower on the farthest planet on the farthest rim of the universe. He had no way to get there. Not from his earliest years did he have a chance. But love found him even if he wasn't able to find love on his own. God's will appeared in letters as bright as neon at midnight saying, "Trust this one. He'll show you where to go." And as scared as he was, he (heroically in my mind) picked up his burden and started walking into his new life, one baby step at a time.

I knew that is what God told this man because it is what He told me when I first saw him. It was during his first few days in treatment. As big and intimidating as he was, he was scared. He was hanging out along the back wall of the huge common room, scowl firmly in place. He looked fearsome. His sign was pretty easy to read: "KEEP THE HELL AWAY FROM ME."

But I saw him. I saw the little boy who never had a father, so never was introduced to his real Father. The distance between us lit up like a river of gold. "Go get him," my old familiar voice said. "Go show him who I am." And I did. And here a few short months later, this same man is terrified to be without this new truth called love that so excites his soul. He didn't find the way to this far distant planet by accident. His Father's will showed him the way. God's will always shows us the way home.

2. The room at home I use for an office is a bit weird, I guess. Years ago I started tacking, taping, and gluing photos I collected of people I had met along the way. My walls are covered with what must be three hundred or so pictures. They are only the tip of the iceberg, but I don't have room for any more. Each photo is a snapshot of a miracle. Each one is the face of God made flesh.

Last night I was sitting in my office looking at the pictures on one wall and remembering. One picture brought me back to a time I hadn't thought of for years. It is of me and a pleasant-faced young woman. Although I can't remember her name, I sure remember her spirit.

We were at a conference in Las Vegas. I was doing a workshop on understanding the nature of untreated childhood trauma in adulthood. I can clearly recall walking up to the room where my workshop was being held and seeing this young woman waiting for me. She walked up with all the confidence in the world and said something like, "I am an island girl from Hawaii. We work with the most wounded of the wounded. We use your material. It helps. I want to tell you that I love you." She was barefoot and wore puka shell bracelets on both wrists.

After my session, a few people hung around to talk to me. All of a sudden, I was looking at the Hawaiian princess standing right in front of me again. She said, "This is how my people share our spirit with people we love," and she pulled my head down and breathed her spirit into my mouth.

Perhaps it was one of those "you had to be there" moments, because in that instant God, who is the source of all love, clearly stepped through the thin veil that separates time from eternity. All these years later, sitting in my dark office holding that picture in my hands, I once again felt God's endless goodness. I felt His words unmistakably flare to life in my spirit once again: "I have you. Relax. You are mine, and no harm shall come to you."

God's will is not brutal. My enemy is not cancer or addiction or anything other than what would worm its way into my response to what is. My enemy is any thought or perception that would allow self-pity, doubt, or anger to infect my spirit. I look at all the good Father has done for me over the long years, how He has guided my feet and filled my life with so many wonders. His will is and always has been blessings beyond measure.

God is good. All the time. No matter what. His will is always to my great benefit. To each and all He pulls us close and says, "Let me show you how I share my spirit with you, whom I love."

I have cancer. You might be struggling with some other burden. There may seem no way out to you. You may feel totally abandoned and helpless at the moment. You may feel there is no hope. You may feel God's will is cruel, is brutal, and is killing you. If so, I urge you to hang on. I urge you to grab ahold of Father in a "Mine" that cannot be broken. God's will is not to torture you. Hang on. The God who makes a way out of no way is as close as your heartbeat. He is faithful. Whether or not we understand what is going on (What? Me? Cancer? Impossible!), hang on. A way will open to something better than we could have ever imagined.

I don't know why such wretched things happen to people. But I know no matter what jumps up to smack us in the face, turning away from God's love won't make it better. No matter what, GRAB HOLD! Hang on! Even now, God is going before us clearing the boundaries, barbed wire, and rusty nails out of our path.

Never doubt it: We are loved. You are loved.

Onward,
Earnie

———

{PAULA} Let me describe Earnie's office as best as I can. All of the wall space is covered with pictures of family, friends, and people we have met along the way. He loved his office and the inspiration it gave him. The floor was covered with projects yet to be done. For him the hardest part about turning seventy was that these projects might never be completed. He put each project/book into a separate plastic bag and stacked them on the floor. People loved seeing his office and were sure he knew what each project was and where it was, but that wasn't really true. He did have an amazing memory, though he was known to say, "Well, looks like I will need to redo that project 'cause I can't find it." Even after we took down about a hundred pictures for the wake and the celebration of Earnie's life, the walls were still covered with hundreds of photos.

Many times through life it seemed like we needed to hold on and trust that our God had something better planned than we knew. I heard Earnie say many times, "We reap what we sow." There were so many times when Earnie and I talked about how grateful we both were that a Twelve Step program had come into our lives. The Twelve Steps are twelve skills, and they saved my bacon oh, so many times. Five years ago I was diagnosed with a tumor wrapped around my spine. The diagnosis took some time, but when I went to the Mayo Clinic, my surgeon told me he had seen many of these and although each was a little different, he had performed hundreds of such surgeries. Many people asked if I was scared then, but you see, I had been practicing turning over what I couldn't take care of "to the God of my understanding" for more than thirty-five years. This is the Third Step: "Made a decision to turn our will and our lives over to the care of God *as we understood Him.* " So I recognized that I couldn't do a thing about this situation, and I chose not to let fear rule my life. Whenever the fear came, and it often did, I turned it over. This is what

I also did with Earnie's cancer during the time we had left together.

It's true that I wondered, "What will my life be like without him? Who will I have to share my daily thoughts with—who, who, who?" When this would happen while Earnie was still alive, I would bring myself back to the now and turn the rest over to my God. I am so very grateful for my faith and for my Twelve Step experience. Through the Steps, my faith has increased and my relationship with the God of my understanding has become more personal.

• • •

ℛound 8

The Wee Hours

October 25, 2010—The wee hours, 2:00 a.m.

So far the most inconvenient aspect of my cancer is interrupted sleep patterns. I often find myself awake around 2:00 a.m., in what I call the "wee hours." It might be inconvenient as far as sleep goes, but it is also a blessing. I like the wee hours. I always have.

In these hours I find that the veil dividing our "normal" world of spirit caught up in our fragile bags of flesh called bodies and the world of spirits freed from flesh thins out. In the wee hours, the rules of "normal reality" relax. Other things become possible—wonderful things that are as real (or even more so) as anything that happens in the flesh.

The actual date I'm writing this is Monday the 26th. What I am doing here is recording what happened ten or so hours ago. A red flag is waving as I sit here in the "cold light of reality" intending to tell you what happened earlier. What seemed (and was) perfectly normal then looks pretty nuts now. At least for many I'd guess that it does. But this is my story, and I'm telling you how it is with and for me.

I knew I wasn't going to get back to sleep at 2:00 a.m., so I went and sat in my office, surrounded by my photos, and looked out into the darkness beyond my window. It didn't take long before, through the thinned-out veil, I became aware of an image looking back at me. I'd seen this image any number of times over the years. I never clearly understood what it meant, but it seemed—from somewhere, for whatever reason—it wanted to come into me again. So I just waited and, sure enough, the image came through the veil and moved inside of me.

I really do mean "moved inside of me." The wee hours' images aren't like looking at a picture in a book or even simply remembering something. It's more than that. The images do indeed take up residence in my consciousness, feelings, and thoughts. It's not *remembering* being there—it's actually being there. It's living and reliving whatever memory or thought or picture comes through the veil. So it was with this image.

The image I've seen so often is a large, powerful eagle sitting at the top of a tree. Its huge body is black as coal. Its head is white as snow, as are some of the tips of its feathers. The eyes are yellow-gold and shine with a fierce light beyond anything born of this earth.

Above this eagle is a tall, wide layer of mist. The mist contains all the wretched, hurtful, tragic things that happen to people. I've seen this mist glow blood-red with rage and fear. I've often heard the howl and snarl and moan of fighting dogs rising in and through the mist. They are fighting for their lives. They've been pushed to the brink and have no other option but to kill or be killed. The mist is the repository of all the tears that have been shed by humanity down the long corridor of our existence. The mist is a terrible place to be. It's even a worse place to be stuck in.

But when the eagle is good and ready, for reasons known only to itself, it spreads its mighty wings, lifts off, and effortlessly rises through the mist. There is nothing in the mist that can cling to it or slow it down. Nothing of the mist can harm the eagle. The eagle is of a different order than anything in the mist. That's the sense that overwhelms me every time I have seen the eagle rise up through the mist—how easy and effortless its passage is. It rises up, soars through the mist, and then disappears into an endless blue sky like a speck falling into the sun.

I've used the image of the eagle rising through the mist hundreds of times over the years in various talks, books, and one-on-one sessions. And I've seen it happen so many times. I guess there has never been a moment in my life when I didn't "know" in some way—far beyond rational understanding, beyond any power the mist ever had over me—that there was an "eagle." There was always something stronger than anything that could hurt me. The solution was always stronger than the problem. I might not have always known what the image meant or exactly who or what the eagle was, but I always knew evil, pain, and loss did not write the last line in the book of life.

So I just sat there watching the eagle take flight again. I just sat with it and waited to see what would happen next. What happened next didn't take long.

In the magic of the wee hours, the image of the eagle rising through the blood-red mist kind of fell apart. It broke into pieces, reassembled somewhere, somehow, and came back through the veil in a whole different form. It was something familiar again, something I'd seen and been part of many times. Of all things, it was like being inside an old film clip of a track meet that happened in 1957. I've been in that film clip many times over the last half century. But for it to make any sense to anyone else, I have to tell you a bit about our track team. We really didn't have one.

At least we had no track, no uniforms except old basketball shirts and shorts, and in a sense, no coach. Our coach was the football coach, who felt it would be a good idea if we had a track team to help keep the football players in shape during the spring. He had no idea how to coach track, so he would walk around during what served as practice sessions reading out of a "How to Coach Track" book.

He ordered the eighth-grade boys to dig a pit in the playground during their recess time. All the while he stood over their work reading his book. When he figured we had a good enough pit, he filled it with sand and we were good to go.

We had one super track star, Dick Hegarty. I don't really know what the rest of us thought we were doing out there. As far as I was concerned, I wasn't fast enough to run any short races, so what was left were the relatively longer races: the 880 yards (no one had ever heard of meters back then), which was twice around a normal track if you had one; or the mile, which was four times around a normal track.

The trouble with the longer races was no matter how hard I trained, or thought I trained, I never got to that point where the blessed "second wind" kicked in. The idea (I guess) was to push yourself hard enough and, if the track gods smiled on you, when you were at the end of your first wind, the second wind started. This would then enable you to stretch out, breathe easy, and finish your race strong. It must be something like the "runner's high" you hear about these days.

Now, the problem was if that second wind didn't materialize when you pushed yourself to your limit, you seized up. This meant you still have a hundred or two hundred yards to go, but your legs are heavy as lead, you feel like you're breathing fire, your vision blurs—it's terrible! You can't quit. No one just quits because they feel like they're dying—you still have to gut out the rest of the race. All you can do is stagger down the track like a gut-shot old horse. It's not only painful but profoundly humiliating.

So the strategy I had—and I wasn't the only one on our team that my father more than once called a "raggedy-assed outfit if I ever saw one"—developed. Since I didn't trust or believe this mysterious second wind would visit me, I would run slow enough that there was gas left in my tank. My thinking was that when it came time to "kick it in to the finish line," I wouldn't suffer the fate of tying up at the end. This strategy saved a certain amount of pain and humiliation, but it didn't do much for making good time.

(Speaking of strategy, at one meet the boy on our team who did the long jump discovered to his horror, while warming up, that he couldn't jump far enough to get from the takeoff board to the pit. They don't even start measuring the length of jumps before several feet into the pit. Poor Pat couldn't make it to the pit. So he figured out that he would pretend he somehow messed up his steps and would scratch all three of his turns running through the takeoff board and on through the pit. That was the only way he got sand on his shoes that day. Indeed we were a raggedy-assed outfit.)

So, about this track meet: It was held in Council Bluffs across the river from where I lived in Omaha. The school was named Thomas Jefferson. (They had a fine, large track. They also had real track uniforms.) It was a large meet with a lot of schools. The meet was called the T.J. Relays.

My race was the 4 x 880 relay—each member of our noble team ran 880 yards. I ran third of the four.

Although none of our team members ever owned up to practicing the strategy of "save yourself so you don't embarrass yourself down the stretch," I suspect we all practiced this approach. By the time the baton got to me that day, it looked like there were a hundred runners ahead of me. I was sure close to last if not the last guy starting out.

I don't know why, but somehow I felt this race would be different. The runners right in front of me must have used the same strategy we often used, since they were hardly going faster than a brisk walk. I couldn't go that slow, so I passed them up. That felt pretty good. So I figured, what the hell, go a little faster but don't push it too hard. So I passed up a few more. That felt good, too. I was paying close attention to the first signs of tying up—a catch in my side, my breath starting to feel like it was on fire—but it never happened. I finished my first lap and had passed maybe half the runners ahead of me. Still no signs of cramping up. What was this? I wasn't tired! My God, was this what a second wind felt like? I felt strong. I felt like I could get going and catch more of the runners in the lead. If this is how good runners feel, no wonder they liked track.

So I kept going. By the time I got on the back stretch, there were only two runners ahead of me. I was still feeling strong. I felt like, "I can do this!" So I pulled up on the shoulder of the first runner ahead of me. We ran stride for stride for maybe ten steps, then his will broke. He knew I was going to keep going. He wasn't willing or able to go with me, so he dropped back. Now there was just one runner ahead of me. I have to tell you about him.

Well, not about him but about the school he ran for. His school was Blair High. We beat them pretty regularly in football, but for some reason they always had top-notch track teams. They were good. They had uniforms and even very, very cool warm-up outfits. Their coach was well known, and he knew what he was doing. For all I know, he might have written the book our coach used. But this boy from Blair was the only one ahead of me; I was on a once-in-a-lifetime second wind and I thought, *Go get him. Run him into the dirt.*

We had about a hundred yards to go. I pulled up on his shoulder—and then my will broke. What I much later came to understand and name "The Lie" reared its head and slammed on the brakes: "Who do you think you are? You can't win a race. You can't beat a guy from Blair. You're going to tie up and look like a fool. Slow down, for God's sake, before you humiliate yourself." Like that— "The Lie."

It was the only time in high school I ever got a "second wind" or had a chance of sailing past the last runner and winning, and I let "The Lie" steal it away. I learned from that, though. Never once in the next fifty-five or so years did I ever let "The Lie" rob me again.

Not that it matters, but the fourth and last runner on my team was a freshman named Billy McAfferty. He was a tall kid with legs like toothpicks. In later years, I heard he got good enough at the 880 to make the state high school meet. But that wasn't 1957. As I look back, I think Billy must have been horrified at getting the baton in second place. He wasn't second for long. He finished about where I started—near the back of the pack. Who knows, maybe he learned something from that race too? Maybe that is how he got good later on?

Back to this morning. I just sat there for a while, soaking in the wee-hour magic. I felt the second wind. I knew what it was like to finish strong.

Presently Father stepped through the veil. I've always known and felt God as the "Unseen Hand" or "The Voice behind the Voice" or "The Love from which all Love comes." But there was nothing unseen about this visit. He wasn't "behind" anything. He came in as who He is— at least as far as human beings can know, even using the wee-hour magic.

I felt held. I felt "Mine." I knew down in that place that matters most that Father had no intention of hurting me. He was with me and far beyond—like how I feel when I am with my guys. We are all CHAMPIONS. And I could-n't be more proud to be with anyone on earth. It felt safe and warm and good.

We sat there for a while. I asked Him, "So how about this cancer thing? Are you going to take care of it, or is it time to ride the lightning to the end?"

After a bit, I heard or felt—or something—Him say, "Look again at the eagle in the tree." And the image of the eagle came back to me. Father said, "See the crows?" And this time I saw a flock of crows sitting in the tree beneath the eagle. They were squawking, flapping their wings, and making all kinds of noise. They didn't want the eagle in their tree.

I said yes, I saw the crows. Father said, "What is the eagle doing?"

I saw the eagle wasn't doing a thing. He wasn't paying the least attention to the crows. It was like the crows weren't there.

"Eagles don't care about crows," Father explained. "There's nothing a crow can do that matters to an eagle. Your cancer is a crow. Don't pay all that much attention to it. I have you. Trust me, when it's time, I'll hold you even closer than I am now. We'll lift off, rise through the mist, and go to a place that is so beautiful you can't conceive of it while you wear your ragged cloak of flesh. I can hardly wait to take you there. When we are ready, we'll leave. Not before. Don't worry about it. You've never been safer."

So that was good. I decided I was going to tell my oncologist the next time I saw him that cancer is just a crow. I doubt any of his medical books define cancer that way.

After a bit, Father also told me this: He said, "You'll never tie up again. You are going to finish your race strong. I'll be your second wind, as I've always been—even when you didn't feel it. This time when you pull up on the shoulder of the last runner in front of you, you'll have all the juice you need to sprint to the finish. Trust me. You're going to love it."

So I finally know why the images of the eagle rising through mist and the glorious feeling of the second wind were given to me again and again over all these years. I get it now.

I was finally getting tired. So many images, spirits, angels, and ancestors I had never met before were crowding into my little room; there wasn't room for one more. It was a great time. I knew I'd be an exhausted wet noodle the next day. (I am.) But it was ever so worth it. Like I say, I really, really like the wee hours. I like the truth of the wee hours.

God is good. All the time. All the time God is good.

Onward,
Earnie

———

{PAULA} At Earnie's celebration of life, his friend Neal gave me a symbolic feather. It will be passed on down through our family.

I believe that one of Earnie's biggest gifts was to take good information that was floating around and put it into a down-to-earth doable format. "The Lie" became a big part of a program that Earnie created and wrote that we called the Life Management Program. It is now offered at the Dan Anderson Renewal Center at the Hazelden Foundation.

If you feel like you are repeating behaviors or are in need of deeper insight, this program will be helpful for you. Personally, I have been through the program three different times and also helped Earnie teach it to different groups through the years. I simply love it and find the format simple to use—not necessarily easy work, but very doable.

The first time I went through it, I remember telling Earnie that this process doesn't work, and he very calmly asked, "Have you written it down?" My response was, "No, but I live with you." I didn't realize the power of writing something down, and when I did, I then saw the pattern.

Here is what Life Management is all about:

> "What we live with,
>   we learn.
> What we learn,
>   we practice.
> What we practice,
>   we become.
> And what we become
>   has consequences."

> — Earnie Larsen

One day one of my Sacred Sisters from my Saturday women's support group delivered some healthy protein balls. She said to tell Earnie she had seen an eagle fly over our house as she turned into our driveway.

The phrase *"God is good all the time. All the time God is good"* are words used down at the Sally. So often I have heard myself saying, "God is good."

It brings me great comfort!

· · ·

Round 9

Purpose

October 27, 2010

Several people have recently told me, "I think you have one more good book in you." "Yeah? Like on what?" I asked one of these individuals. He thought for a moment and then said, "Something on purpose. Like what our purpose is here on earth."

The more I thought about that, the clearer it became: I don't know what anyone's purpose in this world should be but my own. Purpose, it seems to me, had to do with what turns your crank. What gets you excited? What feels really important? What makes your heart beat faster?

That's a lot of different things for different people. Whenever I'd bitch and complain to Gary Weber, one of the true angels in my life, about how irresponsibly people spend their money on "just stuff" while other people were starving to death, he always set me straight. Gary would say that if the people got their money honestly, they had a right to spend it on anything they wanted, and I had no right to complain. It was their money, and they had a right to do with it as they wanted.

Gary kept me grounded. I guess my point here is that different things are wildly different for different people. Purpose is different for different people. And I suspect the reasons why one thing is important to one person and seen as just junk by another goes to the very core of who we are. I suspect purpose is all tangled up with and growing from the most powerful experiences we had as children. It's what life taught us is important, or that we don't deserve, or how best to protect ourselves. I suspect purpose looks backward more than it does forward. Anyway . . .

All I could ever do about purpose is to share what my purpose is, what gets me excited, what feels terribly important to me and what I think must be pursued. I don't know all the reasons why my purpose feels so important to me. It just does. But I know it goes way, way back into my past. And into the past of those who taught me through experience why it was so important.

Curtis is a good example:

I met Curtis a week ago at the Salvation Army after our Friday night class. I noticed he was sitting alone on my right-hand side as I faced the men in the auditorium. He's a white man in his late fifties or early sixties. He's thin, has wispy fading red hair, wears glasses, and looks like a man who has spent most of his life keeping a low profile so trouble won't find him. But his addiction found him, and trouble follows addiction like stink on rotten fish. Just by looking at Curtis, I could tell he was a very shy man who finds it terribly difficult to stand out in any way.

But after class he came up to the front of the room with several other men who wanted to ask questions or just stand there and "yak" a bit. Curtis was going to walk right by me and keep on going. So I stopped him, asked his name, and shook his hand. I asked him if he was new here. He said no. He had been at the Sally for several months, so I apologized for not noticing him sooner and introducing myself. He said, "Oh, I knew who you were. I should have probably introduced myself sooner." That was about it.

Last Sunday just before services began at my beloved First Community Recovery Church, I happened to look back and was surprised (and thrilled) to see Curtis walk in. He stood in the back of the church looking around. I knew he was looking for an out-of-the-way place to squeeze into and not be noticed. So I went back to get him.

I greeted him and told him how glad I was to see him. Then I asked him if he would like to come up front and sit with me, Dockmo, Stu, Jamarr, and a bunch of the guys.

"We're all in the same club," I told him. "We all come from the same place." I waited for him to tell me what he wanted to do. If he wasn't ready to come up front, that was fine. You have to respect where a guy is. But he seemed more than willing to come and sit with the rest of the brothers.

I asked Dockmo to slide on down a seat so we could make room for Curtis. I was on the outside chair of the second row and Curtis was right next to me. Then our great big service started. I'm sure Curtis had never seen or been part of anything like it.

In most churches there are a lot of places to hide. The whole idea in most churches is to go along with the rubrics and not stand out too much. In fact, in most churches a person would feel awfully scared or intimidated if they were asked to stand up and share something from their hearts. Which is fine. I make no judgments on any other churches. It's just not how ours runs.

Our church is rooted in the Black experience of God and the Black experience of service and worship. Not better than, just different from. At least different from anything I have ever experienced in my church career. It most certainly was different from anything Curtis had ever been part of.

Mostly Curtis stayed seated in his chair next to me. He even stayed seated when Brenda, our pastor's wife and the "First Lady" of our church, came singing and praising. Brenda has the kind of voice that worms its way into your soul and makes you want to get up and start moving. Waking up the dead, she walked (really more like danced than just walked) right up to our row. She leaned into our row and with her heart and face in full-praise mode kept singing and inviting us to open up to "God loves you." Then she'd pull back a moment before leaning in again and singing with her beautiful voice, "God loves you." Really, really powerful, beautiful stuff.

Curtis didn't move in his chair. I was wondering what he was feeling—or if he was just blown away. I got a clue a bit later.

There is a part of our service called the prayer call. Everyone is invited to come up around the altar and hold hands or hold on to the person next to them while our pastor or Mother Yates or someone does a prayer from the bottom of their soul asking, in one way or another, that we all remain under the care of God and in deep fellowship with one another. We all know that without both of these things, we don't stand a chance.

Well, Curtis seemed willing enough to come up around the altar. He also seemed willing to hold my hand during the prayer. I don't know who was holding his hand on his other side, but he held mine. Several times during the prayer, when Pastor John Hunter was pouring out his heart that we remain faithful to our calling of standing strong in the Lord, I felt Curtis squeeze my hand. Well, not a real hard squeeze or anything, but something. He was there. His heart was front and center. He was *there*.

I lost track of Curtis after the service. Maybe he got out of there as fast as he could and headed back to the Salvation Army. Maybe he will be at class next Friday, and maybe he won't. I'm not in control of what Curtis does. What I *was* in control of was recognizing him and reaching my hand out to him. I was in control of asking him if he wanted to come up and sit with us. I was in control of inviting him to stand next to me at the prayer call and holding his hand. And I was the recipient of the huge honor of feeling his hand give a little tug as "The Rev." lit up the church with his prayer.

I can't tell you how terribly important it all felt and was, at least to me. It was *important* that Curtis knew he was invited in. It was *important* that he knew he was welcome. And on and on.

I felt good today, so I drove up to a fast-food place to get a salad. The woman at the cash register was as old as I was and nearly bald. My guess is she never thought her life would take this turn—at her age learning to use a cash register and facing the public with no hair. But what choice did she have? If she had other options, she wouldn't be there.

Again, it felt terribly *important* that I somehow tell her how important she is, that I make her feel valued and worthy. This wasn't just doing a "random act of kindness." As good as that might be, this wasn't that. This was like fulfilling a responsibility that your baby has enough to eat or showing up for someone in your family who needs help. This wasn't a take-it-or-leave-it kind of thing. This mattered! This needed to be done! Evil must be confronted.

I well remember my first year as a priest in 1967, when I was stationed in the inner city of St. Louis at the foot of the Pruitt-Igoe housing high-rises. I was at the hospital one day and "just happened" to walk past a window, behind which were newborn babies. I stopped in front of the window, and there in front of me were five tiny human beings shivering because they were going through withdrawal from the heroin their mothers were on. I was overwhelmed by the evil! These tiny babies looked like nothing so much as blue-black bruises. Not that they had bruises, but that they were bruises. It struck me like a hammer between the eyes: What chance do these innocent babies have?

The God of my understanding stepped out from behind the veil at that moment. He stood in front of me as clearly as this computer screen is in front of me now.

He asked me what I thought. I told Him the evil was intolerable and asked why He didn't do something about it. He told me that He was. He was standing in front of me. He asked me if I was willing to join with Him and do something about the evil. I told Him I'd do anything.

That's when He asked me if I would be willing to run into whatever burning house He pointed me to, no matter how dangerous it was, to find other lost children. I'm surprised I knew enough to tell God that I would if I didn't have to go alone. I told God that I didn't think I was good enough or strong enough to keep charging the fire if I didn't have help. He told me that I would never go alone. He said if I was willing to go, then He would always go with me. That's when I fell to my knees and committed to fight evil with Him for the rest of my life, no matter what. "Let's go," I said. We've been going ever since.

I eventually came to understand that "making miracles" was the response to evil my God was asking of me. He was telling me, Don't leave people who are caught in "The Lie." Don't pass up someone who thinks they are unlovable or would not possibly be wanted as a friend by someone else. Don't leave Curtis standing alone, or this aging woman behind the cash register. The red mist surrounds us all. The battle is everywhere, so jump in and make a difference.

For ever so many years, I've made a contract with myself that I would cause, see, or celebrate at least three of these miracles every day. All I had to do was pay attention. Opportunities are everywhere. Then I would list these miracles just to make sure I was paying attention. That's what my God Files are. They are endless stories of how God takes the form of flesh among us.

So back to the woman at the cash register: Outside of starting a conversation with her (I was the only one at her register), I kept asking Father to show me what to do. I wondered, *How do I communicate to her something of her goodness? How do I tell her I don't care if she is old and bald, so am I? How do I reach behind the outside and touch something of the inside?*

She gave me the clue. There were signs behind the counter of several kinds of ice cream they served. I said, "Wow! Look at all these flavors of ice cream." The woman, her name badge said Doris, kind of blinked on for a moment and said, "They are all good too!" Doris liked ice cream, I guess. So I leaned over the counter, like we were exchanging secrets, and asked, "Say, Doris, which of these is your favorite? Whatever you like the best is what I want to try."

And there it was. Like Curtis tugging my hand, Doris's face melted. I got to her heart. If someone wanted to try whatever flavor she liked best, then it must matter what she liked best. And if her opinion mattered, then *she* must matter. Her face at that moment was like a perfect canvas from which emerged the face of God.

Purpose? I guess it is whatever it is. From my present viewpoint of my body hosting a cancer, all the questions sharpen: At the end, what do you want your life to have been about? What do you want to have been important to you? What do you want your heart to have been anchored to? If one doesn't like what those answers would be at the end, maybe it's time to change one's focus of what's important.

For me, when the eagle lifts off rising up through the mist, I'll be happy and proud of what my purpose was. I don't know what else I'd have to say about purpose. If I were going to write a book about it, I guess it would be an awfully thin book.

Onward,
Earnie

———

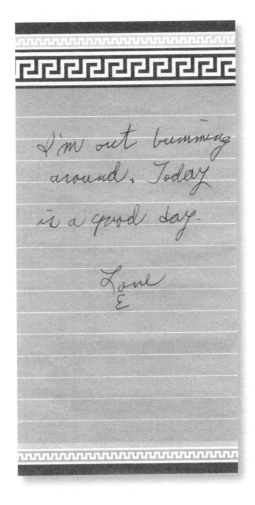

I'm out bumming around. Today is a good day.

Love
E

Through the years, we talked many times of how one thing leads to another. One day in my office, I got a call from a man who sounded like he was from Scotland, but he lives in Australia. He wanted Earnie to speak at their Australian conference, which was going to be a week long. Now, because Earnie always put so much physical energy into his talks, doing talks for a week didn't sound all that good to him. However, this was a special deal, so the two of us went to Australia. During that week, we got to know most of the people attending the conference, including those who worked at the Salvation Army—which they called the Sally. And the story just goes on from there. That was the beginning of his/our connection to the Sally in Australia and, when we got back, his/our connection to the Sally here in Minneapolis. If not for the Australian trip, no Sally here, and if not for the videos, no Australian trip. Now who could have planned all of this?

. . .

Round 10

New Game, New Rules

October 27, 2010

This cancer thing is a whole new ball game. With new games come new rules. One of those rules is, "No, I don't have to do it."

This morning I got up thinking, *I have to figure out a way to get more attention to my latest book on aftercare.* But then the thought hit, *No, I don't. I don't have to do any of it.*

Paula and I had an appointment scheduled yesterday afternoon with our family physician, but it was a windy, dark, and cold afternoon. We had both done something in the morning and were tired. As it got time to go out into the cold, rainy day, I thought, *I don't want to go.* My drill-sergeant voice said, "You have an appointment. You have to go." But then my new voice said, "No, I don't." Nothing is going to happen in this next week that will make a difference healthwise, so I rescheduled our meeting for next week—and stayed in bed reading my book.

I have a stack of love letters in front of me. People I

haven't seen for years have written, expressing all kinds of compassion and love. My immediate thought is, stop messing around and write them back. If they took the time to write you, you owe it to them to write back. But then I think, no, I don't. It would take a week's worth of energy to write them all back. That's not what I want to do with a week's worth of energy.

The other day I looked around my office and saw many hundreds of projects all lined up, outlined, and ready to be made into talks, CDs, and DVDs. They are the collection of a lifetime of paying attention. I said to myself, "I have to get going and get these out before it's too late." Then my other voice, the voice of this new game with new rules, spoke up and said, "No, I don't. If Father wants these projects done, then He'll find a way. Doing projects is not in my job description right now."

Almost every time I turn around, I find it's time to apply these new rules. From my new viewpoint, I see how totally my old rules ruled my life, which was fine—those were the correct rules for then. But now is now, and new rules are in play. It's actually kind of fun learning to play in this new sandbox.

Onward,
Earnie

———

{PAULA} Earnie tried to respond to people quickly if he could. He believed that if someone asked, then they probably needed the help yesterday.

Speaking of help, here is how we got Earnie's letters on the St. Joan's website. I would never have been able to do this by myself. At the end of October, I received an email from the St. Joan's webmaster, Jeff. It mentioned that they were looking for articles for the website. I read it over quickly and dismissed it, since who has time for that? But then I started to think it over, and I thought that it might be a good way to get Earnie's message out to many people. What if Jeff could post Earnie's letters on the website? I checked it out with the powers-that-be at St. Joan's and was given the green light. Then I asked Jeff if he would be able to do this. He replied that he would be honored. Then I told Earnie!

Now here is another interesting part to this story. When I met Jeff at the church, I thought he looked familiar, but I had seen thousands of faces through the years at Earnie's seminars. I asked him what he did for a job, and he replied that he was a teacher in a northern suburb of the Twin Cities—Brooklyn Park, Minnesota. Earnie and I lived in Brooklyn Park. On my way home, I remembered a teacher our two daughters had had for science class in junior high, so immediately I emailed them and asked about a Jeff Rhoul. Not only did they both remember him, but they also remembered the science project they had done for his class. Now that is a sign of a good teacher! We get help in many different forms. Jeff helped us and, in turn, Earnie's letters helped so many other people.

. . .

Round 11

My Dad Left but
My Father Came Back

October 30, 2010

Dear family/friends/team/loved ones,

I love all your emails! Not just because they are filled with love, wisdom, and caring, but also because they often reveal a message from deep in your hearts. My cancer situation seems to "give permission" (if that is the right phrase) for many of you to reveal beliefs and thoughts you might not otherwise share. This kind of sharing is very, very cool.

One of the emails I recently received was from a man I don't know all that well. His name is Paul. He was telling me how much he appreciated my "faith statements." Paul said he had been to a lot of my seminars back in the 1980s and 1990s, so he knew my road had not always been easy. He said he was especially talking about aspects of my relationship with my father when he was still alive in this world. "But," Paul said, "it seems you have made peace with all of that and now have a loving relationship with the God you call Father."

He said he had too. Then he told me this story:

Paul's father had had some kind of breakdown when Paul was a child. As a result, his father had spent many years in a sanitarium or ward of some kind. The father was sent home when Paul was twelve, but he never fit in. He'd been gone too long, much like a soldier coming home from one or many tours of duty in Iraq to find he doesn't fit in. Nothing feels comfortable or familiar. It wasn't long before Paul's father split from the family.

Paul told me his dad called him and arranged a meeting with him—in an alley, of all places. Paul was terribly excited to see his dad again, but he soon learned that the purpose of the meeting was for his dad to tell him he was leaving town and wouldn't see him again. He was simply going to be gone. Then he turned and left Paul's life forever.

Paul is now sixty, and all these years later, he still can't get that picture of his dad turning around and walking away from him out of his mind. That young Paul, speaking now as an older man, said he kept shouting after his dad, saying things like, "Don't leave. Come back. I'll be a better son if you come back. Don't leave me." But his dad never turned around.

Today's Paul told me that after a lot of work and help from a lot of people, he has finally been able to move past the little boy in the alley promising his dad he would do better if he would only come back. Paul said for many years, even as a child, he blamed God for being abandoned. "No more," he said. "Now my God is much like the 'Father' you talk about in these letters."

Then he wrote this beautiful line that I want to record and send on down the line to anyone who might need it. Paul said, "My dad walked away but my Father came and got me."

Again, if Father has me in His arms (saying MINE and holding me close), as He has us all, there is nothing to be afraid of. Crows mean nothing to eagles.

Paul's line was a great gift from God today. It went deep. "My dad walked away, but my Father turned around and came to get me." Love it. Thanks, Paul.

Onward,
Earnie

———

{PAULA} Earnie and I spent much time talking about how real and honest people would get in the emails they sent to him. It seemed the cancer did give them permission to share what was deep in their hearts. What a good lesson for all of us. That is the wonderful part about knowing that you have cancer and that your time is limited—we get real!

So if you have something that is important for you to say to another person, don't wait; do it today. Don't miss your turn and live with regret. Do it now!

· · ·

Round 12

Church

October 31, 2010

I had to miss church today. I just didn't feel up to it. A dear friend was all set to pick me up and take me, but I had to call him and cancel. I hate to miss church. Church to me is like jumping in a swimming pool on a scorching hot day. And this "pool" is filled with love. God truly lives there.

So what I did instead was slowly hold each dear face of our small church community in my mind and heart and pray for them. I lifted them up to the Father, as they constantly do for me. There is no end to the good these wonderful people do, nearly all of it without recognition or the thought of recognition or the want of recognition. They are—as are all good people—the embodiment of God's love on this earth. They are God's skin.

Since I couldn't go to church with them, I brought them to me. We had our own church. Next Sunday I'll feel better and be with them again. I'm already looking forward to it.

If we praise God in the good times, so must we in difficult times. I am blessed beyond measure. God is good—all the time.

Onward,
Earnie

———

{PAULA} Earnie hated to miss church; he was usually there early. It was an opportunity for him to talk with anyone and everyone. First he would greet the deacons as he came in the door; then he'd go check out the kitchen people who were preparing for the fellowship after the service. He might spend some time talking with a particular person, but then was a greeter of all. In nice weather, he would stand outside and greet the guys who came from the Sally and Turning Point Treatment Center, just so they would know they were welcome. Brenda often starts the service by singing "You Are Welcome Here." Earnie said it just touched his heart, and that is the power of music, which goes right to our hearts. His favorite hymn was "Precious Lord"; our friend Sylvia Little sang this song at our wedding, and we all sang it at his funeral.

Now that Earnie's gone, the first Sunday of each month I go to his Recovery Church. This past month, my daughter

Erin and her family all came too. Erin asked, "Do you think Earnie is smiling as he sees us all leave for the Recovery Church, when in fact he so wanted us to do this while he was alive?" I do think he smiles at this. Going to this church feels so dear to me.

. . .

Jump on Fear
and Cut Its Head Off

November 1, 2010

I got a somewhat strange email this morning. This man asked me if I thought I might be in denial over my cancer. He said it didn't seem like I took Stage IV cancer all that seriously. If not denial, he then suggested I might be in a "disassociated state."

Hopefully he will keep reading these letters. I'd tell him, "Hell no, I'm not in denial. I fully realize sooner or later the cancer in me is going to weaken the flesh until it can no longer contain the spirit. I know that. I accept it."

The other thing I am not in denial about is that "I" am more than my body. I'm not in denial about the power of cancer. Nor am I in denial about the power of the God of my understanding—my God has a lot of names. He has a lot of faces. He comes to me at all kinds of odd times. We sit together, talk about old times, and laugh a lot. We look down the road of this phase of my journey and know that it's all good. Knowing I am held in the hand of my

God, it's all good. With Him, what could be bad?

I've always believed that if something nasty is coming down the road at me and there is no chance of escape, the best thing I could do is go out to meet it. Jump on it as hard and fast as I can and cut its head off. Kill it. Pull its teeth and claws so there is nothing evil or bad it can do to me.

Cutting the head off this cancer thing seems to be mostly a matter of acceptance. We keep what we fight. What we won't let go of won't let go of us. It's fear that keeps us enmeshed with the wolf. Fear binds. It burns like napalm that won't wash off. Beat fear and the head comes off the beast.

So yes, I have cancer. One of these days, but not today, or tomorrow, it will kill me. But what is there to be afraid of? I don't fear cancer in the least. Nor do I fear dying when that time comes. As I said before, cancer can't hurt me. It's a crow. I'm with the Great Eagle. Eagles don't bother with crows.

No, I'm not in denial or in fear. What I am mostly filled with is gratitude. My God and I have gone to so many wondrous places! We have seen such mind-blowing miracles. As I said earlier, I've had a front-row seat at Lazarus coming out of the tomb a million times. Each time was thrilling. Each one well worth the price of admission, no matter how high that price might have been. I am grateful beyond words for the life I've had.

Just last night I was part of a team that gave a presentation to a class at a local junior college. A group of us do the class four times a year. The class is about drugs and society. Mostly their textbook is about pharmacology and public health. There's almost nothing about the human face of addiction and recovery. That's what we try to provide. We tell our stories.

I told the professor who lined up the class that I'd do my part of the class as long as I could leave when I was out of gas. He said that was fine. As always, the class was filled mostly with sweet, young faces. Who knows what they hear or don't hear? Doesn't matter. Our part is to tell the best and deepest truth we can.

I didn't stay for the whole class, but I've heard the stories of the marvelous other speakers before. I know what they have to share. Each one is a story of profound transformation—from a man who went through treatment forty-nine times until he finally got it right, to a beautiful young woman who never had a family and started stripping when she was fifteen, to an older woman who has lived with abuse and torment all her life. She told the kids that she was finally through being used. The next time a man had come at her, she said, "I cut him. It took 150 stitches to sew him up. Then I had to get out of town before his friends cut me up."

But that was all then. Now they are years into their new spiritual lives. They don't fear the past and will go to any lengths to help anyone else shake off the demons of fear in their lives.

On my way out of the class that night, I passed the dear lady (and my dear, dear friend) who had cut up her attacker, and as I did, she reached up, pulled me close, and said, "I love you." When a person has that kind of clout, goodness, and power surrounding them, what is there *ever* to be afraid of?

Cancer can't hurt me. I've already cut its head off. Held by my God, I have absolutely nothing to fear.

For the life of me, I don't see how anyone gets through this life without that same kind of connection to Love— love that fans out and blows over the earth like a warm breath of spring.

If you are afraid of anything, don't run. Jump on it and cut its head off. Be done with fear.

Onward,
Earnie

———

{PAULA} Earnie loved giving presentations to this class because he always got to take some other people with him, so they could share in the gift of service to others. We go to give but instead we always get, especially if we share ourselves with another.

Through the years, Earnie and I had many, many talks about fear. I had been in Al-Anon for some time when I remember looking up at the banner with the Twelve Steps on it. I can remember it as though it were just yesterday. I took the word *alcohol* out and put in the word *fear*. I could work with that. Then it became my Program. Before Al-Anon, I thought I was the only person who had this terrible fear and didn't know what to do. Finding out this wasn't true was a miraculous day for me. I credit Al-Anon with saving my life. Fear controlled me and I did or didn't do things out of fear; not a good way to live my life, but I didn't know any differently. Finding my Program remains a pivotal point in my life.

A pivotal point in Earnie's life was the day he discovered that the home his father was raised in was one of a raging alcoholic. I can still hear Earnie's voice coming out of his office saying, "You won't believe what I found out today." After that, many things clicked into place for Earnie like the opening of a lock. His Program became more personal.

• • •

Round 14

The Great Hymn

November 3, 2010

I've talked with God a lot lately. I've spent more time than I usually would walking in the spirit world that is available to me at this time. That's why (I guess) I was just sitting in my office, surrounded by my pictures. I was waiting for one of them to speak up and talk to me. If I'm patient —and receptive—one of those pictures always speaks up and comes in for a visit.

The one that jumped up was an old picture I dearly love. I got it maybe fifteen or twenty years ago while doing a conference in Florida. While there, I was thumbing through a recovery newspaper and there it was. The picture was black and white in the paper, but it was so powerful (to me) that I called the paper and got the name of the artist. I had a wonderful talk with the artist. I asked him if he had a copy of the original that was done in dramatic color that I could buy. He said yes, so I bought the copy. It's been on my wall ever since—a constant reminder of "how it really is."

The focus of the picture is of a concert conductor in a tux as seen from behind. His arms are up, his baton directing the musical traffic that creates what can only be glorious music. But the cool thing is that he is not conducting row upon row of human musicians. The conductor is standing before a lovely lake. Trees fill the sides of the picture. There are rocks and boulders and a brilliant sky. And out of all of them comes energy. They are alive. He is conducting what Pierre Teilhard de Chardin called "The Hymn of the Universe." All things, if we but have the eyes to see, play their part in this Great Hymn. The Hymn would not be complete if each did not contribute their critical part.

Yes, I believe nature has a powerful song to sing, as was depicted in this picture. But, to me at least, nothing comes close to the power and beauty of "ordinary people" standing up and singing their song of life. It is we, standing in the light of God, who create abundant life for our fellow travelers. We are the God-sent angels who are to do battle for all the souls around us who don't know how worthy and beautiful and powerful they are. It's us. We are the ones who are sent.

As I sat in my chair listening to the picture on my wall, a glorious, endless procession of battle angels began to file past. These were people who in all truth were and are more angel than human, though they wouldn't say so. But whether they would or not, it is still the truth. Nowhere is God closer to human beings than in human beings.

Jinny, who manned the Twelve Step intergroup phone forty years ago in Grand Rapids, Michigan, walked by and waved at me. She's on the other side now. No matter. She was an early mentor of mine, though I doubt she knew it. She was old when I knew her—and heavy. Her forearms often were bruised from leaning on the table she worked at during many a long hour on the phone. But then a solution came, she said. "My boys stepped up and took care of it." They made her a kind of sheepskin rest for her arms. She loved her boys, but God help them if she called down to the club for someone to go out and help a suffering alcoholic brother or sister who had just called and no one responded. I can hear her as clearly as if it were yesterday, storming, "Someone was there for you when you needed help, so by God, you had better be ready to go get someone else."

Oh so many, many, many people walked by the window of my soul! Past and present. All part of the Great Hymn. All doing their part in glorious anonymity. I just sat there with my spirit, heart, and mind wide open. I felt like a child at his first parade. The wonders never seemed to end.

I could list a hundred who walked and danced and marched past me as I sat on the curb, watching in awe. Each one a story of incredible music rising up from the very rocks and rivers of their lives. Each one a story worthy of being told if only time and energy permitted.

One of the emails today asked me, "Are you really not afraid? How can you not be afraid?"

I'm not afraid. I am far too busy watching and listening to the Great Hymn being set in motion by the Conductor to have time for fear. I'm in the middle of the Hymn. The beauty of the music surrounds me. It lifts me up. Hearts turned to stone melt in this music. They learn for the first time the meaning of soft. And then they, too, join the great cavalcade going forward, bringing light and grace into the world.

Who do you see walking past your window?

Onward,
Earnie

———

{PAULA} This picture, *The Great Hymn*, hung on the wall of Earnie's office. He told me someday it will be Johnny Mac's. He is a music man. I just shipped it to Johnny last Saturday, and today I am writing about the picture. I didn't remember that the picture was to go to Johnny until last week. Earnie had written an email to John maybe a week or two before he passed. It was the last time Earnie had come down to his office and mine. The email was saved as a draft and that still amazes me, since he really didn't know how to do this. I had read it many times but couldn't make out what Earnie was saying. However, about two weeks ago I reread it, and then I knew. It referred to the picture on his wall in his office. His office walls were covered with pictures; it was like a cave with all of these wonderful faces, your faces, beaming out at him. They so inspired him.

. . .

Round 15

Inside the Shabby Box

November 4, 2010

Today was not a good day. I only got about an hour's sleep last night, and that always means the next day is going to be like dragging a five-hundred-pound anchor up a hill. I don't know why I couldn't sleep. It felt like I had fifty cups of high-octane coffee in me. Who knows?

What I do know is how important it is to praise God and keep pushing through, no matter how I feel. Anyone can praise God on the mountaintop. The question is are we— or am I—as willing to praise Him in the valley? It's one thing to say "Yes, Lord" when my sail is full, but what do I do when the wind dies down and all that's left is to row for the distant shore as best I can?

"God is good" when His spirit fills my lungs and I run without getting tired. And "God is still good" when my lungs burn and it's hard to put one foot in front of another.

It's when the road gets rough that it is important to hold form.

So my God, my Father and Mother, my Spirit and Friend and Guide along the way, today was tough. I could only move along like a gut-shot workhorse. I'm sure it wasn't pretty. There were a dozen things I wanted to do for You today. I wanted to make something beautiful for You. I wanted to make a difference in the fight. But all I could do was try to keep my own nose above water.

I ask You, Father, as always, to see the intention behind my poor effort. My intention was to lift You up. I put that intention like a piece of perfectly shined malachite or a dazzling opal inside a rough cardboard box. That was all the energy I had. I ask You to look inside the box. Throw the box away. Keep the prize. The prize is for You.

If there is any good or benefit You can derive from my cancer in the divine economy known only to You, You are welcome to it. If it can somehow help someone else climb out of a dark hole, reject whatever lie was pounded into them, and reach out for the truth of Your goodness and love, then take it. You are welcome to it. As Brenda sings with such beauty, power, and passion each Sunday, You are welcome here! My house may be falling down, but You are welcome here.

A man called today to remind me of a pharmacology class I had agreed to speak to in two weeks at the University of Minnesota. I told him the best I could do was get some other men who would do a great job for him—and if I could, I would make it; and if I could do some of the sharing, I would. But I told him I never know what my energy level is going to be from day to day, so that was the best I could do for him.

It struck me as odd—as so much of adjusting to a life with cancer is odd—that after all these years of doing endless talks, it has come down to this. I'll show up if I can, and if I can't, I won't. Life is leave-taking. Everything ends.

But standing up or sitting down, talking or not talking, running or just wobbling along, may it all be a beautiful stone, Lord, that You find inside the shabby box.

Onward,
Earnie

{PAULA} Earnie often used rocks in his talks, and for sure he loved collecting them. Once we were in Albuquerque, New Mexico, for a conference and Janee Parneq took us to Santa Fe for the day. We had a great time. In one of the stores was a large (seventy-plus-pound) rock of malachite and azurite. It was simply beautiful. Earnie's eyes were caught with it, so after we walked out of the store I asked him about it. I said if I had wanted it, he would have encouraged me to get it. So when we got back home, he called the store and bought it. Even today, it sits in our living room on a stand. Earnie always wanted to learn how to cut it and make things from it. That was not to be, but the rock is still there.

By the way, Earnie was able to give the talk. He was a most dependable person. If he said he was going to be there, he was; if he said he was going to do it, he did it. The limitations of cancer were a huge adjustment for Earnie. There are so many lessons to be learned here for all of us. Earnie showed up and did what he could and then had to let others carry on. We learn about our slogan "Let go and let God." We aren't in charge of everything, only our part—and we do the best we can.

. . .

Round 16

The Best

November 6, 2010

Another not great day today—not bad, but not too good either. It feels like I'm walking in wet cement. So, time to make a decision. Stay where I am, focusing on the inconvenience and frustration of my situation, or pick up my ball and go play somewhere else?

Last night we had a great class at the Salvation Army. I did it on how "Anyone can shout alleluia on the mountaintop, but what do you do when you get caught in the valley?" Anyone can run like a champion when they have a lot of wind and feel strong. But what do you do when your lungs turn to fire and your legs feel like lead? Anyone can have a great plan before they climb in the ring to fight someone. But what do you do when you get smacked in the face for the first time?

The point was that all of us have reasons to quit. We all have reasons to lie down, letting our spirits and attitudes be eaten by spiritual vampires like resentment, fear, anger, self-pity, and shame. But it's always a choice. We have a choice about our spirits and attitudes no matter what. Lie down to be eaten by vampires, or get up and run down the road so fast the vampires can't catch us. It's a decision.

What I decided to do (at least for today) is move on. I went to that place that never fails to pick me up and blow air under my wings. My attitude was, screw cancer. Cancer is what cancer does. So be it. But I have more important places to go and things to do than cancer can touch.

So in my mind, I went back to class last night. I went back and saw and felt again the glory of God manifest in the transformation of lives, the transformation of those I will always think of as "my guys." I fixated on them. I stopped time, rolled it back, and melded it again into what I not only saw last night but was so honored and privileged to be a part of.

If I looked hard, I imagined I'd come up with a dozen events—things that happened; what was said; the look in the eye of one of the men; body language that said, "You got me. I'm paying attention." An event is a happening. It's a miracle. It's Roman candles going off. It is a great and important event taking place in as humble surroundings as Christ being born in a stable—and none the less glorious for that.

An event is simply, for me anyway, paying attention to The Best—the very Best that life on this planet has to offer. I can't saturate my body and soul into that ocean of grace and not be lifted up. So the decision for me becomes simple: Endure the death of a thousand small cuts, which cancer seems so far to be for me, or jump into that ocean of grace that is God, going toe to toe with all the evil that would turn us from eagles into crows. I jumped.

I want to list two of the events I am talking about that took place last night and truly lifted me up. These are the kind of events I have stuffed into my God File over the years. But, right now, I'd like to share them with you. I want you to know what I am talking about.

As I said, last night's class was about giving glory to God no matter what is going on in our lives. It was about holding form even when you are being chased by dogs. My point was that we all make countless decisions during the day that define who we are. We have to earn our souls every day by the decisions we make. We become our decisions. For better or worse, we are what we do.

I talked about gratitude. When is there not room for gratitude in our lives? When has God not shown His loving hand in our lives? When has He not been there when we cried out in pain and terror? If we were willing to listen, the Father was always there to hold us up. No matter what is going on in our lives, no matter what kind of a fix we are in, no matter how helpless or hopeless we are tempted to feel, God is. God cares. God is there for us. No matter what, declare MINE, and hang on for all you're worth.

So I did my spiel to the 130 or so men there. There are always some "old-timers" who come to the class. These are alumni who come back to give testimony that ongoing recovery is more than possible. When I was done with my stuff, I asked if any of the old-timers wanted to come up and share with us how they handled tough times. Several did. Absolutely amazing! I want to tell you about one.

"Ike" (not his real name) got up and told us he was two years clean. He was a longtime heroin addict from California. Ike was also a big-time felon who worked for the cartels and had spent twenty-five years in prison.

What he told the group was that he had just heard from one of his "soldiers back home" that there was a $250,000 price on his head. He told us his first inclination upon learning this was to round up some of his soldiers, go back to his hidden store of C-4 and automatic weapons, and "get them before they get me." But God stepped in, the weight of all the new decisions he had made over the past two years cut in, and Ike said he realized he couldn't do that without putting a needle back in his arm. Ike said there was nothing in all this world worth getting back on the needle. So he just let it go. "If they want me, they know where to find me," he said. "What happens, happens. I'm good no matter what."

Ike and I have rubbed souls throughout those two years. A good bit of who we are has rubbed off on each other. I am part of him and he is part of me, and we both live in the hollowed-out hand of God. Our journeys are joined together.

It's The Best, at least for me. Some would say, "Big deal, so one druggie blows up another druggie. Good riddance to both of them."

But that's just the point—there is only one druggie in the story. Ike is different now. He's not that old druggie anymore. He's a changed man. He doesn't live for drugs, money, and violence today. No, today he lives totally for going into his version of the burning house to bring out others who are trapped where he was.

Yes, it's a little thing. It's the story of one man accepting the gift of grace and transforming his life. But once you "get it," there is no such thing as "little." Once you cross the line into seeing with spirit eyes any and every transformation, it is as big and magnificent as a medieval cathedral. It's just The Best. And to be given the opportunity to play some small part in that monumental, miraculous transformation is just The Best.

Then, sitting right there in the front row (as he always does) was Jamarr. He often carries around a large bundle that looks like a big Bible. What it is, though, is his book. He's writing the story of his life called *Going from a Street Thug to A Man of God*. Jamarr knows whereof he speaks.

But last night, he didn't have his big bundle. He had a rather large plastic bag. I asked him what he had, and he showed me a big red Tickle Me Elmo doll. I asked what he was going to do with that.

Jamarr said he bought it off the toy pile in the sorting room at the Sally. He said the five-year-old son of a woman he used to know was in the hospital suffering with leukemia. Jamarr's daughter died a year ago from leukemia, so he wasn't going to miss this chance to bring some joy and companionship to this little boy.

The fact that Jamarr saw this, understood it, and took action blew me away! I know a bit of his story as the "street thug." Oh my, in spades! But there he sat, in the front row, no thug clothes or bling, a new man, transformed. Here he was, on his way to lift up a desperately sick little boy.

I held up Elmo so everyone could see it. I walked up and down the aisles with it. I was probably hollering and pounding the words (I say probably because at those times I have no awareness of what I am doing or how I am doing it) "Do you *get* it? Do you all get it? *This* is the fire in the boiler. This is the front-row seat at a miracle. This is what all the decisions are about. Not just 'What's in it for me?' but 'How can I place even one brick in this New Jerusalem we are all called to build?'"

I don't know who "got it" and who didn't. My job is to do the pointing out of what it is all about. Whether they get it or not, or when they get it, is up to a Power higher than me.

Here is where I probably went too far during class. At times it feels necessary to act out what I am talking about, like hugging Malik and proclaiming "Mine!" I was talking about the need and benefit of making a gratitude list no matter what is going on. I thought—or the thought came to me—*okay, let's do it now.* So I told the men, "If you want to show your gratitude to God for all the gifts you've been given, hit your knees. Get down right here and now and let's pray."

I got Jamarr, Jeff, and Stu, who were in the front row, to help me get down on my knees—I hung on to them so I wouldn't fall over while praying—and they lifted me up when we were finished. I wanted to show the men, my Champions, that if a guy as old and sick as I am would get down on his knees to say thank you, then there never is a time when we should hesitate to do the same.

It was the right thing to do, but it sure burned up all the energy I had.

As I sit here right now, many other events from last night pop into my head. I see them. I feel them. But even being caught up in The Best, I also feel my back starting to hurt as well as my neck. It's time to end this and move on. I'm way ahead of the vampires now. They won't catch up to me for a good while.

(One man came up after class to tell me something. He was so very scared. He looked like someone had tried to cut his throat. He wanted to tell me that he felt "the spirit of encouragement" coming from me and wanted to thank me for coming out for the class, "even though you are looking death in the face." I told him NDY—I'm not dead yet. What do you imagine this man's story is? The events just keep coming and coming.)

Enough for now. Church tomorrow. I am grateful, more grateful than I can ever say. I wouldn't trade my life and all it has been and done to me for anything. Whether on the mountaintop or in the valley, I praise God. God is good—all the time, no matter what.

Onward,
Earnie

{PAULA} I took Earnie to the Sally for the Friday night class. We ended in prayer. I was in the back of the class and, therefore, the back of the group. What a sight to behold! Talk about your miracles. Earnie always said, "Our worst stuff becomes our best stuff if we hold it up to grace." Here were men who in society's eyes did wrong—and they did— but now they were on a new page, and the possibilities of whom they could become, whom they had the power to reach out to, were endless. I would pick Ike for my team any day.

On November 7, we went up north for a couple days to Duluth, Minnesota, which has always been one of our favorite places. There it became quite obvious to both of us that we were not going to have two years together. Our time was going to be shorter—maybe, in fact, much shorter.

We tried to do many of the activities we usually did in Duluth, but this time we were quite limited. So while Earnie took a nap, I went across the street to see what the shops in Canal Park had to offer. When I came out of the dress shop with two new tops, I clearly remember feeling very relieved. But why? It was then that I realized why: I could wear these tops for a funeral. The tears streamed down my face, so I walked over to the water to watch the gentle motion of Lake Superior.

After we returned from Duluth, the two of us spoke of the time limit and what it meant. Earnie had tears again around the fact that he had called the "guys" from the Sally out to trust someone and now he wasn't going to be there for them. Earnie became committed to using his remaining energy to connect with people. He so believed in community for all of us.

I have been so very grateful that neither of us were angry or in denial about what was to come.

. . .

A "Little Good"

November 11, 2010

There is no such thing as a "little good."

I was very much looking forward to seeing Jamarr at church on Sunday. I wanted a report on how it went when he gave the little boy with leukemia the Elmo doll.

Jamarr didn't look joyful though. He said the little boy couldn't say "Tickle Me Elmo"; all he could say was "EMO! EMO!" Jamarr said the child had tears in his eyes. "His daddy ran out on them a long time ago," he said, "so he ain't used to anyone giving him presents." Then why the sad face? Jamarr said he went back to see the little boy the next day. He wasn't there—he had died during the night.

Jamarr was so sad, so that inner voice in me that never seems to sleep told me to tell him something. I let this good man know that Father told me the little boy was marked to pass on a day earlier. He, Father, went inside the child and kept him alive and breathing because the child needed to know what it was like to get such a fine gift from someone he didn't even know. God wanted the boy to experience the gift. Then, when he had, Father and the boy went home to a place beyond the reach of cancer or anything else that hurts.

Hearing this made Jamarr feel better, I think. I don't know where the words came from. I never know where they come from. But I saw Father breathing for the little boy, and I saw them journey on together.

Right now my shoulders ache. My stomach hurts a little too. My energy level is on Empty. None of it matters all that much. Yes, I ache a little, but I also got to see Father loving his children. I saw those two rise up together. I got to witness a self-described street thug offer a sick child he didn't even know a drink of living water. Compared to the Glory I see all around me, my little aches and pains don't matter all that much. They are swallowed up in the Glory that surrounds us all.

Onward,
Earnie

———

{PAULA} Earnie was so touched by Jamarr and what he did for that little boy. We are all called to do different things, but each is equally important!

Now, here is a wonderful experience that happened to me after Earnie's passing. I went to the Recovery Church for the fourth anniversary celebration, and many members of our family joined me. Toward the end of the service, there is a special blessing for those who want prayers, and they come forward. Our friend Jamarr came forward to sit in the designated chairs. Loren (our eighteen-year-old grandson) leaned over and asked me what that was about. In the Recovery Church this is a common ritual, but in most other churches it is not. So I told Loren and his brother, Josh, that Jamarr was up there for special prayers. Just after I said that, I could feel Earnie's right hand on my shoulder, squeezing it and encouraging me to get the boys and go up to put our hands on Jamarr's shoulders and support him. So we did. We all had a lot of tears, but it was such a dear time. You see, Jamarr had decided that he was going to go back into treatment at the Sally the following day.

Back in the summer, Jamarr mentioned that he would love to hit some golf balls, so Earnie asked Loren if the three of them could go out and hit balls one day. Loren said, "Of course." So off the three of them went to hit golf balls. When they came back, our grandson Josh was rollerblading in the garage and shooting hockey pucks. Jamarr watched him, fascinated. The four of them just hung out together.

On the way back to the Sally, Earnie asked Jamarr what the best part of the day was and he said, "Everything, but especially just hanging out in the garage with your grandsons." By the way, this man is writing his story and calls it *Going from a Street Thug to A Man of God*.

Jamarr has started a "Shoe Ministry" in Earnie's name specifically for children. My family and I witnessed the power of the Shoe Ministry at church last Sunday. He had rows of shoes for the children to try on. He asked them first if the shoe fit and then if the color was what they wanted. He had been collecting the shoes for a couple of months and had asked anyone who could to go down to the Sally to buy a pair of shoes and then donate them for the children. Wow!

. . .

Round 18

Never Say Never

November 14, 2010

Last night we had our first big snow, and with the snow came a situation I've been dreading. We've lived in our house for twenty-five years. Every one of those years I parked my car in the driveway so Paula could have the garage for her car. We have a neighbor plow our driveway, but he has a lot of clients, which means that many times over the years I have shoveled around my car so I could get in, start up, and drive away. Sometimes the shoveling is nasty. Minnesota winters can be rough.

The snow was wet and heavy today. I had a medication at the drugstore I needed to get, but I just didn't feel up to going out and getting it. So Paula, a guardian angel who never lets up, said she'd do whatever shoveling needed to be done to go get the meds.

It goes against my grain 10,000 percent for her to be out shoveling while I sit inside! I hate it! There are a hundred men I could call and ask to come shovel so Paula wouldn't have to, but that would take time. Paula wanted to get going. So she shoveled, ran the errand for me, and said it was no big deal.

I just can't believe how little energy I have. Maybe that's true for everyone with cancer? I'm like a battery that can't hold a charge. By far, the worst aspect of cancer for me so far is this lack of energy. I'm doing all the nutritional and supplement therapies I know how to do, but nothing has made much of a difference so far. So, we'll see.

Most of the afternoon I spent reading the book of Job from the Bible. He had a lot of bad things happen to him. He lost all that he thought made him important. He complained to God about it. God's basic answer was that Job, a human being, wasn't capable of understanding why God did what He did. God's answer was for Job to do the best he could with the cards dealt him and leave the big picture to the Divine Mind.

If I don't find "an answer" to this lack-of-energy issue, it's pretty clear that the vast majority of things I did all my life are at an end. I even had to cancel out of my Friday class at the Sally yesterday. I'm only hoping I feel good enough to go to church tomorrow!

But all the "old normal" things like giving talks, writing books, going to groups, doing DVDs, creating programs, etc., are over. Right now, there is nothing of this I am capable of doing.

The Twelve Step program I love so much says, "All it takes is all there is." It says, "Half measures avail us nothing." I guess none of us change, or open up to a greater possibility, unless there is absolutely no possibility of retreat. We have to burn our ships on the beaches so we won't be tempted to sail back the way we came.

Maybe that is what Father is doing for/to me. Maybe I never would "let go" until I was forced to, which this cancer seems to be doing. Forced to move from "doing" to "being." Forced to just "be" and feel the arms of Father around me. I don't like being forced. But maybe that is what proves the need. If I could jump in my boat and sail it back where it came from, I'd do it in a second, but then I'd miss the lessons taught in the cancer classroom.

I feel bad thinking of all the big and little things Paula will have to add to her already full plate. I feel like a big old lump lying on the couch while she is out shoveling. But there is nothing I can do to change it. Never in a million years could I have foreseen such a situation—Paula out shoveling and me staying inside! Lesson for the day: Never say never. And also writ large in brilliant letters: All it takes is all there is.

So pray for me and pray with me that I learn all the lessons set before me. We're calling the oncologist Monday to see if he has any suggestions for this lack of energy—

maybe another blood transfusion. I told my fifteen-year-old grandson, Josh (who puts up with my goofiness), that I was going to use blood from the world's strongest man contest. He rolls with it all. He knows it's just Grandpa being Grandpa.

God is good all the time. Maybe Job will visit me in a dream and tell me what he learned.

Onward,
Earnie

———

{PAULA} Life is not always on the terms we would like, and that sure was an adjustment for Earnie. I suspect it is for most of us.

• • •

Round 19

Ain't No One Mad but the Devil

November 15, 2010

Dear companions on the journey,

I find many of the (wonderful) emails I'm getting are from folks who are fighting their own tough battles. Many of them express gratitude to me for sharing my journey through this cancer mess.

I'm thrilled if anything I share in these letters is a help to anyone else. A few years ago, Paula and I did a Life Management Program for thirty or so women. They weren't qualified in any way—meaning they weren't alcoholics or in Al-Anon, etc.—they were simply a group of thirty women like any group of women you'd find anywhere. As the weeks rolled on and the women became more comfortable and trusting, it was amazing to discover how much pain they were carrying around inside their spirits! Their sharing again confirmed that we need to be kind to everyone, because everyone is fighting a tough fight.

Many of us who have taken up this fight against our hurts and wounds seem to be the type A, hard-charging, get-out-of-my-way kind of people. Ever so many of you mentioned finding help in my brother Bill's suggestion to lie in bed and imagine we are held in God's loving hands, rather than see ourselves as lazy or weak because we just can't get up and "get going."

I think of how many of us so badly need to slow down and give ourselves a break. We so need to practice self-compassion rather than self-contempt. Only those of us who are chased by the red-eyed beast of "get going" know how subtle and insane (when we stop to look at it) the impulse to "get going" is. And it all feels so "normal." And it is our normal because that's all we've ever known or done or received strokes for—if carrying one bucket of cement up a hill is good, two is better.

As I've said in these letters, the worst part of cancer so far for me has been the loss of energy, which of course creates the perfect storm:

1. No energy means
2. I can't "do," which means
3. I'm not "doing my duty" and
4. I am therefore a failure.

And the only place for failures is the scrap heap.

My head knows that the above model allows zero space for the lesson(s) about us being more than what we do, about how others can and do love us no matter what we do or don't do for them, about how the only real "failure" in this life is not allowing others to love us. My head knows this, but there can be a huge distance between head and heart.

So, what would it take for me to stop and learn these lessons? Only one thing, I think, and that is being laid low forcefully enough that I can't say yeah, yeah, and keep doing my old normal. And being laid low is what I have now. Cancer is one hell of an anchor! No matter how powerful my old normal is, it's not strong enough to elbow my cancer out of the way. If I'm willing to pray to Father, "Anywhere, anything, anytime—you point where you want me to go, and I'm hard after it," then I have to accept that the loving God of my understanding has a right to say, "Okay, we're going to a different spot than we've ever been before. You won't like it, but it is what you need to learn." And here we are in this whole new ball game called cancer.

"So what's the lesson?" God asks.

"That cancer is stronger than I am."

"No it's not," says God. "Cancer is just another speed

bump. What the speed bump is made of isn't important. What's important is that you slow down and learn."

"Learn what?" I ask.

"Exactly," says God. "You tell me. What are you learning?"

"I'm learning what powerless means. I'm learning there really is a time when I can't take another step. I'm learning I can't do anything, and it bugs me. I'm learning I can hardly get out of bed most mornings, let alone lead a charge somewhere. I'm learning I'm not of any use to you in the fight you started so long ago."

"Whoa," says God. "Tell me that again. You aren't of any use to me in my fight. Is that what you said?"

"Yes. What good am I to you lying in bed trying to pony up the energy to roll over? I'm sick and weak and out of gas. I can't go anywhere, let alone into a burning house. I can't even begin to tell you all the little projects lying around that I just can't do—phone calls, letters to my men in prison, emails to answer, meetings to go to. I know it matters! Me making contact with them matters. It's all part of taking the fight to the enemy. It would matter to them to hear from me."

"You forget one thing," says God.

"What?"

"It's my fight. I call the shots. I till the field. You are an aid to me, but you are not me. You came through the hell of the red mist so you would know what being knocked down so hard you didn't think you could get up was like, but the red mist has no claim on the Eagle. The Eagle goes where it will."

"So?"

"So, the burning house you are to run into now is your own. Someone is dying in your house. I want you to go find all of you that has been lost over these long years. You have been on battlefields of such dark power they made you tremble. You've been to so many ugly, ugly, and dangerous places in my name. You fought for the souls of my lost children a million times over. But this is a new battle. It's time."

"I don't like it."

"I know you don't, but it is what is necessary. Left to yourself, you would never slow down and learn of me."

"But I do know of you. I've seen your power transforming lives every day of my life. I know you. I've seen the miracles. I've seen your face emerge in lives that once were ruined. I've seen you come for everyone."

"For everyone but one."

"And who would that be?"

"Yes, who would that be? Let's talk about that. . . ."

* * *

The above little bit I call "dialogues." They can go on forever. My God Files are filled with them. I find writing dialogues helpful in many ways.

The above dialogue grew out of the fact that I had to cancel my class Friday at the Sally. I didn't make church yesterday, either. I'm supposed to teach a class at the University this Wednesday. Cancel, cancel, cancel. I can hardly do a thing.

And there is a lesson, I guess, forced on me: It's God's fight. I work for Him, not the other way around. He can use me full of cancer and fatigue, "doing nothing," as well as He could if I were up and around. I'm just a dollar in the collection plate. Father is free to use that dollar any way He wants.

All it takes is all there is. All we can do is keep pressing on through as best we can, whether we think we are making any difference or not. All we can do is surrender ourselves into the love of God and say, "Whatever."

People can use these letters any way they want. No secrets. But especially to those who, like me, have been "do-ers" all their lives, I say, let's take a break. Let's just stop, listen, hear the music coming out of the very rocks and trees, and know that Father loves us as well as anyone else. In His hands we are safe. In His hands nothing can touch us. First, and above all else, we are loved. I am loved. I am in the burning house. I am the one in need of being found.

And Father comes to get us like golden rays of light through a gray sky. Whatever speed bumps life throws at us, from cancer to lost relationships to any other flavor of "the unthinkable" that might jump up and smack us in the face, God is there. We are loved. I am loved. All we need do is "claim God" as our own. Grab hold of our MINE with all our power. Cancer is just a speed bump. Father is what the journey is all about. He is MINE.

And as the saying goes at our church, "Ain't no one mad but the devil."

Onward,
Earnie

———

{PAULA} Earnie and I taught his Life Management Program to my Saturday morning women's group. He called them the "Sacred Sisters." This name came from a wonderful group of women out of Detroit; we had worked the same program with those women some years previously. What an experience it was for all of the women in my group! And the benefits to the group were unbelievable. I am most grateful that we did the program three summers ago. The effects have changed so many lives and will continue to do so.

The God Files Earnie referred to were a way for him to record "How or where I saw the face of God today." He used to say if we pay attention, we always see, but many times we are rushing around too fast for this to happen. He recorded almost daily. What a sense of hope to know and feel we aren't out there alone—that our God is right here with us, probably much more than we would ever think!

I now use Earnie's God File for our monthly newsletter on www.changeisachoice.com. So his message goes on and on.

. . .

Round 20

Just Stop

November 17, 2010

All my life I have made it through hard times by using the same coping technique. I call it "just ten more steps." I created it as a young guy mixing and carrying plaster or cement for my dad or my uncle. The buckets were too heavy. The bags of plaster or cement were too heavy to lift. The sand and water it took to mix the cement in the beat-up old box were too heavy to manipulate.

But there wasn't a choice. Quitting or saying "I can't" was never an option, so there I was caught in the middle of "It's too heavy" and "I can't quit." What was I to do? It might only have been 9:00 in the morning, and I had all day ahead of me to mix and carry, mix and carry, mix and carry. So I made up a way out.

No matter how far I had to carry the buckets or push the wheelbarrow, I'd tell myself, "Just ten more steps." You don't have to go the whole distance. You only have to take ten more steps. Take ten steps. And when you've done that, take ten more. Enough ten steps and sooner or later the day ends.

I guess that doesn't sound very sophisticated, but it worked. It has worked my whole life.

There were times after some long seminar out of town when all I had to do was walk on the plane, sit down, and get back home. I recall one such time in Atlanta. After the seminar, I was totally out of gas—every part of me hurt. I made it to the airport and was leaning against a pole of some kind, waiting to get on the plane. Problem was, I really didn't know if I could walk all the way to the plane. I didn't know if I could tolerate even the minor crowd that all plane boardings create. I seriously thought about missing the flight and just sitting down and resting in the airport till the next day. Surely I'd be strong enough to get on the plane then without any problem. But that seemed too much of a hassle.

So I pulled out my handy "just ten more steps" ploy. I didn't have to make it all the way across the boarding area. I didn't have to make it all the way down the Jetway or down the aisle to my seat. I only had to make it ten more steps. And there never was a time in my life when I couldn't make it just ten more steps.

And there is the problem. As long as there was never a time I couldn't make it ten more steps, there never was a time when I was forced to *stop*. If I could make it even one more step, then there never was a time I couldn't struggle on alone.

Then came cancer. For the first time in my life, "just ten more steps" doesn't work. For the first time in my life, yes, there is a time when I can't take even one more step.

I recorded in a previous letter that I had to pass up my Friday class at the Sally. I also had to miss church. Both of those events are dear to my heart. But no matter how hard I pushed myself, no matter how firmly I told myself, "Just take one step—just stand up and take one more step toward the door," I couldn't. I was out of options for the first time in my life.

Life is about learning our lessons, I think. Every event offers a lesson. So I sat back down among all the termites that cancer seems to be—termites eating the house down from the inside out—and asked, "What's the lesson here?"

What came back—like some giant echo from a thousand years ago—was just, "*Stop.*" Stop beating yourself out the front door. Stop beating yourself at all. Stop making a game out of exhaustion. Stop throwing yourself away like yesterday's garbage. Just *stop*.

Then what started to emerge from this new place were voices and feelings that were different to me, different in depth. I had heard all these voices before but never to the depth that *stop* seemed to be allowing.

Every time I miss church, Sister Denise calls telling Paula and me that we were missed. She tells me that I am loved and that the whole church is praying for me. She tells me to stay strong. She tells me our God is a miracle worker and always comes right on time.

Back when I had "just one more step" in me, I could listen to the love and compassion and caring from this spirit-filled woman and say, "Very nice. Thank you. I get it." When in fact, I didn't get it at all. Not really. Not to any depth.

But this time as I listened to her message, it struck me with power: She really does care. The church cares. I am loved. I am more than the number of buckets I can carry, no matter how many steps it takes. If it takes cancer to knock me down hard enough to hear and feel this, then I consider it a good deal.

Paula has been a true angel through this cancer mess. She takes my cancer far more seriously than I do. There is nothing she won't do to help me or make my path smoother.

From the position of *stop,* I saw her in a different light, I guess. Paula is not my nurse or hospice care worker. She's my wife, and she really does *care*. It *matters* to her that I am sick. And, yes, I'd do for her anything she would do for me. But that wasn't the point. Keeping score missed the whole point. Regardless of anything, she was telling me she loved me. And to be honest, I guess the deep, broken button she was pushing was that through her love, she was telling me that I was worthy of being loved.

Until I hit *stop,* I had no way to hear that.

My pastor, Johnny Hunter, called yesterday. He just wanted to see how I was. He said he was thinking of me and felt a hole inside of him.

Johnny and I have talked on the phone a thousand times, but this was different. I guess I was different. I told him how proud I was to have him for a pastor and how blessed beyond measure I felt to have been led to our church. Never could I have guessed the blessings that waited for me there.

We told each other that we loved one another and that we would "Stand on the Battlefield Until I Die." (That's a hymn we often sing at church.) The conversation was the same, but it was also different. I don't even have one more step to take. I don't need to take any more steps. I just need to *stop* and let the grace that surrounds me fill me up.

Last night a dear old friend named Gary called. He was excited. He was calling from some prayer group he saw advertised and decided to attend. Apparently they are connected to other prayer groups all over the country. Gary wanted to tell Paula and me that "tomorrow seventy-five thousand people will be praying for you." It was important to him that we know that.

It would be easy enough to say something like, "That sounds like Gary," or, "Wasn't that good of him to do?" But it was more than that. Gary, who isn't the most emotionally free man in the world, wanted to *tell us,* "Look, I love you. I did this for you. I want you to know how much you mean to me. I want you to *hear* what I am saying."

I do. Differently, from being forced to *stop.*

I could easily list a dozen more such events, but I am starting to hurt. And since I am trying to learn to "stop beating myself out the front door," I'll end this letter here.

I think there are a lot of people like me who make it through the day by staying crazy busy and disassociating themselves from anything that gets too close emotionally. I get it—I really do. But I want to tell you, as terrifying as it seems, until we *stop,* there is no chance all the love that is chasing us can find a way in.

Now I'm really tired. I hope some of this makes sense.

Onward,
Earnie

————

{PAULA} Many times we talked about the lessons we were learning here. My read on all of this was that Earnie was to learn to accept love. My lesson was to learn to ask for help.

After Earnie passed, I had all the grandchildren go through his clothes for anything they wanted and then through his office for the same reason. Through the years both of us talked to the grandchildren about going on an adventure. Life is so much of an adventure. So even after he passed, our Adeline said she so loved going into Grandpa's office because it felt like she was going on a treasure hunt. She has always had a way with words. Once when she was younger, Earnie and I went to pick her up, and Earnie asked her what her mommy told her for the day. Adeline replied, "No whining, no crying, and good attitude." We were still laughing about those words later that night. Adeline came into her parents' room one morning and said, "Mommy, my face hurts so much from crying 'cause I am so sad about Grandpa dying." She is seven years old. Then in comes Isabel, who is five, and says, "No, I am not so sad; *no*, I am not. He was sick for a long time." After the funeral weekend, Isabel asked her father if she and Adeline were sober, and her dad explained all of this to the best of his ability. Then she yelled up the stairs to her older sister, Adeline, "Hey Adeline, we *are* sober." Sometimes when I am very sad, I think of her dear words and it lightens my heart.

Every Wednesday, I pick up the girls from school at the bus stop. Soon after Earnie passed, Adeline said to Isabel, "Quit talking about Grandpa or you will make Grandma sad. Grandma, does that make you sad when she talks about Grandpa?" And I said, "Oh no, Adeline, if we *didn't* talk about him, that would make me sad." She smiled and said, "Oh, okay! Isabel, you can talk about Grandpa, then." Out of the mouths of these babes comes such wisdom.

· · ·

Round 21

You Have to Know the Code

November 20, 2010

Attitude is a choice—sometimes a hard choice, but a choice nonetheless. I struggled a bit with attitude today. It seemed I just couldn't keep my mind in that place of hope and gratitude where it needs to be. Then a beautiful memory floated into my mind. It sat right in the middle of all the mess and said, "Come over here and sit with me. We'll be fine."

The memory was when my oldest grandson, Monte, was about three and Loren was just a baby. We messed around more than any three kids I've ever known. I guess that is why my sister Carol once said, "The only difference between you, Loren, and Monte is that you have change in your pocket and can drive." I thought that was a fine compliment.

Ever-vigilant Monte noticed that anytime anyone hit the digits on our alarm code when going in or out, it made a beep noise. He liked the beep noise. So it got whenever he wanted to do something fun, he would walk under the alarm pad on the wall above him, reach his hands up, and say, "Lift. Lift."

It probably wasn't the greatest idea in the world, but what is a Grandpa going to do? So I'd lift him up, and he'd plunk away at a few of the buttons, making his own beeping noise.

My memory was about such a time when Monte was playing with the alarm buttons, except this time he hit the buttons in a way that set the alarm off. Anyone who has heard an alarm like that knows it is loud enough to wake the dead—or terrify a child.

Little Monte grabbed me as hard as he could. He buried his head in my shoulder. I could feel his heart beating faster than a hummingbird. The poor little guy was a million miles out of his ability to turn the alarm off. The alarm was totally beyond him.

But I knew the code. I could turn the alarm off. No big deal for me to do, so I did. I told him Grandpa could take care of all this noise, no problem.

I bet I told Monte a million times during this stage of his life, "Nothing bad is ever going to happen to you if you are with Grandpa." Of course, terrible things could happen to him, whether he was with Grandpa or not. But most of the things that bothered him or that he wanted (like turning off the alarm) were well within my power. I was trying to ground him in the belief that someone who loved him always had his back. I was trying to nurture a sense of safety in him.

Anyway, as this memory floated into my troubled mind, a voice came with it. It sounded like my voice talking to the scared little boy all those years ago, but it was different. My voice was about turning off a simple code—child's play. The alarm in my head, though, was about cancer, and "how much time left?" and watching my body more or less fall apart. Those things didn't seem like child's play.

But my voice said to me, "It's child's play to me. As you have loved your grandson, so I love you. As you would turn off the offending code for him, so I will take care of it for you. Your heart is beating fast. You exhaust yourself thinking about the future. Forget the future. I am already there waiting for you. And I tell *you*, "Nothing bad is ever going to happen to you, if you are with me. Relax, I know the code too."

So I called up big Malik in my mind and spirit and we did a *Mine*. And all the bad old noise stopped—just like it did for Monte when I punched in the right numbers all those years ago.

I offer up the biggest, fastest, squishiest prayer I can for anyone who reads these words that you know what to do to turn off the alarm. If you aren't big enough to reach the keypad (and none of us is alone), may we all turn to the One who is.

Onward,
Earnie

———

{PAULA} It is December of 1994; Earnie, Montgomery, his parents, and I are out at the Mall of America with Loren, a baby at the time. Montgomery says he wants to go on the log chute ride. His dad says, "Maybe Grandpa would like to go with you." So the two of them get on the ride and after it starts moving, Montgomery says, "I don't want to be on this." Well it was too late to get off, so Earnie zips Montgomery in his brown leather jacket and sits ever so close to him. As they start down the log chute, Earnie later said it was like God stopped the ride, tapped him on the shoulder, and said, "Just as you protect him, I protect you; just as you hold him, I hold you." I, not knowing what is happening on this ride, buy a picture of the two of them and have it put on a mug for Earnie. What a teaching moment for him! We never know when or how we will learn something so important in our lives.

I have said so many, many times as we traveled this road how grateful I am for my faith, for my years in a Twelve Step program, and for learning these skills. Turning things over to a Power greater than ourselves has saved my bacon so many times. I can worry and be fearful, but that is a choice for me, or I can turn it over and do my part. I never knew that before Al-Anon and the beauty of the very spiritual Steps came into my life. God is good! Like Earnie said, learning the code to turn off the alarm so the bad old noise stops is a skill that the Twelve Steps teaches us.

. . .

Round 22

Dear Mom

November 22, 2010

Dear Mom,

I'm not sure why you are on my mind so much lately. Maybe it's because of all the lovely emails coming from people telling me how I "shared my spirit" with them— and that it helped. None of them know you, yet were it not for you and all the gifts you gave me, I never would have reached out to them. So much of whatever I had to share with them was you reaching through me to them. I just want to thank you.

We've talked more since you left this earth than when we were both on this same plane. Sometimes the veil was so thin between us, I could see your eyes looking back at me as I sought you. This was especially true that one night when your presence was so apparent, I raised up my hand to you and asked you to squeeze it or let me know in any other way that you were really with me—that the closeness I felt with you was not just my imagination run riot. And you did. You let me know.

You were one of the very bravest people I ever knew. Your courage astounds me when I think of it. You never quit, especially during those last years when you were so hurt, used up, and limited. But you never complained. You took what came to you no matter how "unfair," stared it in the face, and carried on with such grace and nobility.

I think of all the years you lived with chronic pain from your stroke that ended up in thalamic pain syndrome, and I wonder how you did it. Then there was your mastectomy. Then your eyes started to fail, leaving you to read only with a magnifying glass. And always the congestive heart failure and the hardship of living alone.

Yet your attitude never wavered. You carried on with a positive attitude, putting your best foot forward, and even writing your first book about what you learned along the way. You reached out from your ever-shrinking circle to help anyone you could.

Only once through all this pain did I ever hear you comment about the price you paid to go on with nobility; you told me, "I get so tired of being brave."

Living well is not cheap or easy. Bravery is always the cost in one way or another. It takes bravery to stay rooted on one's square no matter how bad the storm. And you did, right up to the end.

Because of your congestive heart failure, you always slept sitting up in a chair in your tiny TV room. When your grandson Steven found you the morning after you had moved on, your body was lying flat on your bed. Somehow during that last night you were given permission to move on. Enough was enough. I've so often thought of how that might have happened. Did the Lord you loved so much come into your room and invite you home? Or did someone else you loved so much come through the mist to accompany you across that last step? Was it Dad? Did he come to you all cleaned up and shining brightly? Did you both then go on together?

My time is fast approaching. I see death in my reflection. When it is my time, I ask you to come get me. You and Dad. Not that I will be scared or doubtful (I hope), but I want to put my arms around you both and have you do the same. I want to go forward with you. I want everyone who is there, or will be there, wherever we go, to know that we are family. I want to be with you and for everyone to know how proud I am of coming from you.

Wait but for a moment. I am close on your heels.

I cherish you,
Your son Earnie

{PAULA} Over the years, Earnie and I talked about what actually happens when you die . . . nobody really knows. When my good friend Nell was nearing death, she had a wonderful experience of two women coming for her—but she wasn't quite ready, so she sent them back. I suspect when you die young and have young children, as Nell did, it is very difficult. How does a mother or a father get ready to leave their young children? After one of Earnie's good and dear friends passed, his wife told us that just before he died, he had greeted his mother and his sister. So for Earnie, it was going to be his mother and his father. In his final letter to me, he said when it is my time he would come for me.

The best part of this letter is that like most people, Earnie didn't have a perfect life by any means. It is so easy to think that everyone else's life is so much better than our own. He acknowledged that his mom and dad did the best they could. Was it perfect? No! When Earnie began his journey with PTSD (post-traumatic stress disorder) work back in the mid-1990s, he went to a psychologist who told him he had PTSD. Earnie replied, "You are crazy; I have never been to war." And she explained, "That is the problem—you have been to war every day of your life, only you didn't know it." Then she said, "You need to look at your life through the eyes of an abused child." Again, it was like the tumblers of the lock fell into place and the door started to open. About a year ago, he wrote me some pages, saying, "Subconsciously I never let my mother count emotionally in my life. She was there and I loved her, but mostly she never mattered because she wasn't there when I most needed her."

But this letter that he wrote to his mom reveals the change that had happened. What an amazing time that was for both Earnie and me, and what gifts came as a result of him working through so much of his childhood. It was a very painful time. Many told him, "Let the sleeping dogs lie," yet the sleeping dogs were no longer sleeping. He used to say, "Not everyone has it [PTSD], but those that have been through the sustained abuse as a child need to do another level of work." Things did change for him, but it was a very slow process. He loved the movie *A Beautiful Mind,* which portrayed John Nash's struggle with schizophrenia, because the three people who were part of Nash's hallucinations were still there at the end of the movie, but they were no longer controlling him. To Earnie, it was a great example of what PTSD is like—it is always there, but it doesn't have to control one's life.

• • •

Round 23

What of the Ones Left?

November 23, 2010

Trust has always seemed to me the hardest virtue to acquire, because trust is proven by risk. If there is no risk, no skin on the table, then there is no need for trust.

Yet trust is the key to all that is best in this life on earth. What more builds a soul and gives such confidence and satisfaction as moving past doubt and isolation to that splendid state of being where you *know* you are not alone? Others have found me worthy (whether I can see it or not) enough to stand with me, to hold me up, to see the beauty in me that I cannot see myself. They hold my soul in their hands. I trust them completely. Everything they do is for my good.

Trust, of course, reaches out in endless directions. As I sit here tonight tapping out this letter, a rather different aspect of trust has its hands on me. But it is of burning importance to me.

As I see the finish line of my race rushing up to meet me, a huge question burns as brightly as a forest fire. What about my people, Lord? What about my guys? What about all the people I have called out of the darkness in Your name, telling them, "I know how hard this is for you. I know the heroic sacrifice you are making, but trust me. Trust me. I will never drop you. I will stand with you till the end."

I know this sounds arrogant. Who am I to think I ever would or could make such a difference in someone else's life? But it doesn't work that way; at least it never has for me.

I *know* God works through people. I *know* God sends us to work miracles in His name among His people. I *know* many a precious soul has found the Light, who is God, because someone, an angel wearing flesh, showed up and was willing to go through the hell of the red mist with them. I *know* this to be true.

The magic is in the relationship. Donating to a food bank or writing a yearly check to help the less fortunate is one thing. A good thing. It helps. And, of course, the less fortunate can use all the help they can get. But that's not where or how the miracles happen. That's not where the battle is and the blood is spilled and Armageddon is fought on a daily basis. The battle is not about one and done. The battle is about staying put in front of the fire, as long as it takes, until someone lost in the darkness hears the never-imagined words filter down to them: "You are loved. You are worthy. You are forgiven. You are a champion."

And like newborn kittens first learning to open their eyes to the light—whether these people are doing life in prison or caught in some other inner prison behind bars stronger than steel, still terrified beyond words—they respond. They inch forward. Against anything they have ever known, they reach out. They dare to entertain even a flicker of hope. It is the first day of creation. It is a brand-new sun peeking over the rim of the world.

Some would (and probably will) call this just fanciful words, poetry rather than reality. But they are wrong. I've been there. I've seen the miracle start. I've seen and been part of the greatest force on the face of the earth. And that is the power of unconditional love to transform a life. I've seen the face of Christ appear in the devil's front room. And as this glorious emergence takes place, the same refrain in one way or another is always present: "Don't drop me. If you would call me to come out of my tomb, then it must be our sacred covenant that you will stand with me through my terrible new birthing."

I understand that covenant. I have ever since I raged at You to *do something* in front of the window in the hospital of those newborn babies suffering heroin withdrawal, and You said You were doing something. You were asking me if I would spend my life fighting for those who had nothing. Ever since that moment, I understood the covenant of relationship.

So what now, Lord? What of those I have invited out who are half-born? They are just emerging. They are jumping back and forth about whether to hope or not—whether to imagine that anything so grand as a life in the Light could ever be for them. And I am leaving. Not of my own will, but leaving all the same. I called them out for You and now I am leaving.

And so trust. I am exhausted. I have no more words to write. All I can do is throw my soul into the vast expanse that You are, Lord, and trust that You will take care of them. You will keep them coming. You were with them before I was. You love them more than I.

I am done.

Onward,
Earnie

———

{PAULA} Earnie started going to the Sally on Friday nights many years ago to do a program for the guys and to the CRC (Christ Recovery Center) on Wednesdays to their sing-along. It was supposed to be a once-a-week event, but for Earnie it soon turned into more than that. He began dropping in more often. Not necessarily staying long periods of time, but connecting with the guys. It is in the connection that the trust grew.

. . .

Round 24

True Thanksgiving

November 26, 2010

I was looking forward to Thanksgiving with my family members who were in town. We were all going to go to our daughter Erin's in the afternoon. But as the day got closer, I became more certain I wouldn't be able to make even this trip. I didn't feel sick or in pain or anything. It's just that months on end without a full night's sleep, plus not taking nourishment for weeks at a time, would make anyone too weak to do anything but roll over in bed. I just didn't have the energy to go, even though these are many of the people I love more than anyone on earth.

So at about three o'clock on Thanksgiving Day, there is a knock on the door, and here comes Erin's family, the whole family! They had loaded up the turkey and all the trimmings and brought it to our house so they could spend some time with Grandpa.

Four of our six grandchildren are from this family. They are all hockey players, even sweet girl Ella, who at twelve is a force to be reckoned with on the ice. I've been deeply,

deeply involved in the lives of her three older brothers—Monte, nineteen; Loren, eighteen; and Josh, fifteen—from the very start. They are part of the deepest fabric of my being, as I am of theirs. We've had secret names, hand signals, jokes, and crazy stuff from the start. We have taught each other the meaning of God's name.

Even though my sickness is hard and frightening to them, it is important that we spend as much time together as we can. I seem to be awfully weepy these days. A dozen times while they ate, I could have broken into tears just looking at the beauty and love around the table and all that it meant. In the end, all I could do was sing "Alleluia" in my heart and wonder at the goodness of a Father who has given me so much.

God is good. All the time.

Onward,
Earnie

———

{PAULA} A knock on the door, and then in came the troops. How can one not be grateful when this happens? By this time, Earnie was eating very little, but the present was not the food but those who brought it. Our son-in-law said it was what made his Thanksgiving!

The connection with our family through the years has always been so very important to the two of us. Then these grandchildren started coming along and *Wow!* I knew it would be good, but I didn't have any idea it would be this good. Grandchildren love all of us and have room in their hearts for us all, no matter who is biologically related to them. It is an amazing gift!

I came to our marriage with two young girls and a dog. I always had the gift of my two daughters, but all that was new for Earnie. He loved it, however, and in turn it probably had a greater changing effect on him than any other event in his life.

. . .

Round 25

Glory, Family, Love

November 29, 2010

People have a lot of ways to measure the success of their lives. I guess it all depends on what a person considers important. Yesterday, Sunday, I was given such a shot of what matters most to me that I felt like one of the apostles Christ took with him up the mountain. There they witnessed what today we call the Transfiguration. They saw the Glory. Not surprisingly, they said, "This is great! Let's stay here forever." Of course, they couldn't. It wasn't their time yet. They had some hard times coming, so I guess Jesus wanted to give them a peek of why staying on their square during those hard times was worth it. That's how I felt yesterday.

Paula (God bless her!) packed me in the car, and off we went to church. Amazing miracles, at least to me, started going off like flashbulbs as soon as I got in the door. Like what?

The first person I saw was a young woman named Linda, all dressed up, looking like a bright new penny. Last time

I saw her was three weeks ago, which was the last time I was at church. She had just gotten off a bus from Chicago and somehow found our church. She was a mess then. She was sitting on a chair against the back wall like a wounded, terrified child. Linda was coming off some hard drugs, and they were beating the hell out of her as she left them behind.

Someone took her in the kitchen area and got her something to eat. As she ate her cereal, I sat down next to her to just talk a bit. She communicated the best she could. Lots of times in situations like that the best thing you can do is be quiet and just send "You are safe here—You are loved—I love you" messages directly from one heart to another. Mostly that is what I did.

But I did make the plea to her that she return to our church. I told her the big secret was *keep coming back*. Linda needed a place to stay as well as all the basic things people need to survive, like food. I thought there was little chance she would make it back. Her addiction wasn't through for her yet, and there are so many cracks to fall through.

But there she was yesterday, bright as a spring flower! Her face lit up when she saw me, and she came running to me with a huge smile. Linda told me she had been waiting for me every Sunday because she wanted to tell me all the wonderful things God was doing in her life. She was clean, had a place to live, and, she said, "I've found a family in this church."

Like I said, a miracle. I put in this beautiful little bit about Linda because when I started this letter, I had no intention of recording it. But I guess it wanted to be told. A dozen miracles like that happen every week at my church. Anyway . . .

Next, I went back to the kitchen to see if Abraham was around. Diane told me he wasn't and that he had called her to tell her he wouldn't be there this week because he had a paying job he needed to do. Paula and I went up to the front row of chairs. I told her we needed to sit close to the end of the row because I knew I wasn't going to make it through the whole service, and I wanted to make as little fuss as possible when we left. So there we sat, pretty much alone.

All of a sudden I felt a motion beside me. I look up, and there is Abe. He tells me he wasn't coming today, but then he had a feeling I would be there. With him was our great friend Michael T. He was in the wind for a while, and I didn't know if he had come in from the cold yet. We all hugged like survivors from a war. I whispered into Mike's ear, "Are you back?" He said, "Yes. Besides, I needed to come see you."

Then who is standing right next to them but Wardell? He and I had spent a lot of time together over the summer. He's a young man who had just finished fourteen years in prison when I met him, but the glory of God shone through him like the first day of creation. He'd run into hard times, failed to stay connected, and slid back down the throat of the beast of addiction. I kept track of him through the street guys. Dear Wardell was lost. I knew he was being eaten alive with guilt and shame. But there he was, Lazarus coming out of the tomb shining like the sun.

On my best day, Wardell could break me like a stick. All the guys could. But on this day as he leaned in, I hugged him so damn hard I thought my arms would break, if not his back. "Are you home, Wardell?" I asked him. "Are you back?" He said he was.

My friend Jamarr was there as well. Beautiful Jamarr, who had found it important to get the Tickle Me Elmo doll for that sick little boy a while back. We were all there. Gerald came up. So did Brian and Stu. I had to sit down. Abe was to my right. I was awful weepy. I told Abe how I missed him and all the other guys. Abe spent twenty-five years in prison, so he knows all about isolation. But he is three years clean and sober now, and so also knows the joy and endless treasure of true fellowship. He just patted my now-skinny leg, tears in his eyes too, and said, "We miss you too."

Then I feel these two strong hands on my shoulders from behind. Michael T. leans in close and says into my ear, "The family is here. Your family is here. Can you feel them?"

It was then, once more, that I knew what was important in my life. Beyond anything that can be bought or sold, stored or counted, here is what makes my life successful. Standing there (well, really, sitting there) surrounded by men, champions all, who refused to stay down no matter what life did to them. These are truly the lions of God.

A bit later I was leaning forward in my chair with my elbows on my knees. I had my eyes closed. My palms were open and up telling Father I was open to whatever might come. And all of a sudden I sensed someone standing right in front of me. Boy, was there ever someone standing there!

Brenda was standing right there, and God chose to make a cathedral out of her vocal cords. No one can sing like Brenda! And that is what she was doing. She was singing a hymn just to me. She had her hand on my head and would rub it down the side of my face—singing to the Lord the whole time. I only looked up at her once. When I did, she was staring right in my face and was singing the words "And God will protect you."

And my, how my God has. Cancer is just cancer. It's no more than a crow, a speed bump along the journey. And even with that, Father has surrounded me with the hedge of His lions—such mighty men and women of such strength, compassion, and beauty. My soul would have to be blind beyond telling not to see how the love of God surrounds me.

But the deeper part, the part of me that neither cancer nor anything else of this world can touch, that is where Father comes to sit with me. There I am protected, protected as Brenda's hymn proclaimed. There, Father tells me over and over, "Don't worry about it. Don't sweat the small stuff. We are on top of what counts. Do your best. Hang on. And when the eagle lifts sailing through the red mist, that is when the fun really starts."

When we left church, Abe and Mike walked us out. I couldn't have had a better honor guard if two archangels were standing at our sides. In fact, as far as I am concerned, they were.

God is good. All the time.

Onward,
Earnie

———

{PAULA} A few days ago I went to the Recovery Church for the Sunday service. It was the church's fourth anniversary, so of course we had a meal afterward and there was Linda, serving the food. She had made jambalaya. It was food good enough for the gods—what a gift.

Linda told me the story of how she and her boyfriend, who is now her husband, had found their way to the church through an old friend of theirs. Earnie had slipped them a little money that first day and she told me, "We have never been broke; we have been down to $1.50, but never broke."

*   *   *

On that day when the "guys" started to come up, we were so surprised. We thought they weren't going to be there, so it felt like Christmas to see them and to share in this wonderful service with them. Brenda's words rang out loud and clear. God is good! I felt like this might be one of the last times, if not the last time, we would be at the Recovery Church together. Earnie's time was drawing near; we felt blessed to have so many of the men we love so dearly there.

After Earnie passed, Wardell called our house. Our daughter Cara happened to answer the phone. When she finished talking with Wardell, she came into the living room and said, "We need to get something for our Wardell and others as a remembrance." And that is how the idea of the marble was born. Here is what the sign next to the marbles tells all of Earnie's guys:

The Marble

Did you know that a marble is an object originally used to help one remember someone or something important in life? The marble's circular shape is a metaphor for life . . . the round shape reminds us we are all one; the various colors assure us that we are all unique; and the size, although small in stature, when placed with other marbles creates great beauty.

Earnie's goal was to ensure that people were connected and felt a part of a larger community, no matter where they came from or where they were headed.

We ask you to take a cobalt blue marble in honor of Earnie and know that you are never alone, you are held in community, and Earnie is with you always!

When Cara went to buy the marbles, the woman at the store said she was sorry but she only had one color left, cobalt blue. That was Earnie's favorite color. Cara said, "I hear you, Grandpa, loud and clear." (She and Erin both called Earnie "Grandpa" as the children did.)

Many people have come up to me and said, "I carry my blue marble." Our grandson Loren was just at a graduation party the other day, and one of his St. Cloud coaches came up to him and said, "I've got my blue marble in my pocket this very day."

• • •

Round 26

The "Sob Machine"

December 1, 2010

There seems to be a direct emotional feed these days between any experience of deep, genuine love and my "sob machine." There is no question of even trying to hold it in or stopping it. When the button is pushed, the sobs start.

It's all good. I welcome it. To me, it is a sign that even if my body isn't working, the part of me that connects to God is love, and love is all that counts in this life. Both are still in working order, or maybe getting in better working order. Maybe that is a hidden blessing of my cancer.

I'd like to list three of these "instant sob" events—all manifestations to me that God is good and never stops pushing for our spiritual growth to get back to where we were meant to start from.

1. Loren is my eighteen-year-old, second-born grandson. He is tall, handsome, observant, and intelligent. Loren always pays attention. Loren plays hockey for Hill-Murray High School. Last year as a junior he played varsity, went to state with the team, and won a varsity letter. He's

rightly proud of his letter and super proud of wearing his new letter jacket with the sign of his accomplishment right out front.

To understand what winning the right to wear a letter jacket like Loren's meant, I guess you'd have to have gone out for a big team, got knocked on your head day after day, got knocked down a million times and got back up a million and one times, run into the boards, gone up against boys bigger and stronger, and still not backed down. It really is a huge achievement of spirit and skill to win the right to wear a letter jacket. I was always so proud of Loren. I loved how he looked in his jacket and how proud he was to wear it. THIS IS ME, it screamed. AND I COUNT.

Well, over fifty years ago my mother decided to start saving little clippings of things going on when I was in high school in the '50s, things like game scores, write-ups, school programs, and announcements. All these memorabilia got put in a box, and eventually that box ended up in a bottom drawer of the chest in our bedroom, mostly forgotten and seldom to almost never looked at—until one night last week.

I was rolling around, not sleeping, trying to pass time, waiting for dawn. I happened to pull out that old box and sort through the ancient content. Among other things, my mother had pulled off the symbols from my old letter jacket and attached them to an old piece of thick yellow paper.

It immediately sprang into my mind from someplace deeper than conscious thought or decision making: *I wonder if Loren would ever want (or be willing) to put my old symbols on his jacket?* It seemed unfair to even think about. A letter jacket is a supreme symbol of "I did this," but something terribly powerful was welling up in me, wanting to at least ask if my grandson would let me join him in this way.

So I asked. I made sure he didn't feel pressured one way or another. But when I finally got the request out (sob machine on red line), Loren immediately and fully said, "It would be an honor." I felt honored and loved by his gesture more than I can ever say.

(This letter is unfinished. It will probably stay that way.)

———

{PAULA} Loren had Earnie's football symbols put on his jacket and of course wore it the next time he came over—this is one observant grandson. Earnie was thrilled to see Loren in his jacket with the new symbols. For as long as I knew Earnie, he was always into symbols, but he wanted symbols to really mean something. He would encourage people to check out what meaning something represented to them. Then the symbol was a thing of beauty, even if it was just a rock.

When it came time to cremate Earnie's remains, I asked the four oldest grandchildren to each pick something to be cremated with him. Earnie had asked me to do this before he passed. Of course, Loren picked one of the football symbols. We reap what we sow!

Earnie had helped Loren find a car. One day after his Sunday visit, Loren was backing out of our driveway when I flagged him down. I told him that Grandpa's initials, EHL, were on his license plate. None of us had realized this before.

Here is an entry about Loren from Earnie's God File, written about a dozen years ago:

Loren Can Hear Forever

Loren was born into a tough spot. Being the second son born within fourteen months of an older brother is no picnic. Sibling rivalry is guaranteed; so is the fact that the second born for many years will be the smaller, weaker combatant. At least, it usually works out this way. Special attention to the second born pays dividends for a lifetime. It seems there just can't be enough affirmation and support given them, especially in those critical early years.

Loren is one of my grandsons. I love him dearly. If at all possible, I make all his events, all his games, all his school activities. I want him to know Grandpa is always cheering for him. Always and everywhere.

Not long ago he had a hockey game. At five years old, their games are not exactly the Stanley Cup to anyone but them. We have a standing joke that at this age they spend more time on the ice than the puck does.

I couldn't make this particular game, so I wrote a note to Loren and had Granny take it to him. The note first of all had some of our nonsense in it about how Loren was "the man" and to watch out that he didn't get going so fast his skates would catch on fire and melt the ice. (He knows he can't go that fast, but he likes thinking about it. Well, at five maybe he isn't quite sure if he could go that fast or not. I like to get him thinking maybe he could.) Then I told him to listen real hard and he would hear me cheering for him way across town.

When Granny got home and was recapping the game for me, she told me Loren told her he could hear Grandpa cheering for him from all the way across town.

Maybe if children can hear those cheers when they're five, they can hear them the rest of their lives. And if they can't hear them by then, maybe they never will, no matter how surrounded by love they may be. Grandpa is cheering for you, Loren. He always will be.

. . .

Round 27

Oncology Report—
Good News, Not-So-Good News

December 2, 2010

Since you are family, I want to give you the report from my last oncology meeting, but I think it is best understood in a certain context. You know me: There is always a back story. And knowing me, the back story isn't "normal." Anyway, the back story starts here:

My dad was my hero. He was always a giant to me. He was a strong man with huge powers that came natural to him. I doubt if he ever knew or thought about the power he controlled. I don't think he was introspective in the least. Many of those powers were great, good things that kept him constantly united with what was real and important in life. He lived in the heat of the flame of life—and that flame burned bright.

He gave me gifts that went to the core of who I am. Any good thing I have ever been able to give anyone else has his name on it as well. There is nothing good in me that has not flowed through him first. Somehow beyond any doubt or reason, he was sure beyond question that he and his clan were "the best that ever was." To be in his clan was to sit at the right hand of God. And that's all I've ever told anyone else all these years—"You are family. You are the best that ever was."

Not all of his powers were benevolent. There were also huge portions of him, just as powerful, that were sore wounded. Knit into his deepest fabric were the violent lessons he grew up with that set life lessons in the hardest concrete, saying things like "When the battle comes (and the next one is already at your heels), you are alone. Do not ask for help. No one is there to help you. So get tough, hunker down, ride it out—and when possible, attack. Kill the enemy every way you can."

The longer he lived, lacking any insight or idea of how or why to change, his demons rode him like a wet horse. They rode him literally to death.

He taught me what he knew, both good and not so good. I have inherited a box of crazed warriors who live deep within. They never stop trying to take control of my bus and go find a war to fight.

But I do have a way to understand what is going on inside me. I know who they are. Through long years of effort and practice, I've become pretty good at putting them in a box with a sign on the door saying, "Relax. The war is called off today." When they get antsy, I know how to cool their jets.

A week or so before the oncology meeting, I must have really been asleep at the switch. It dawned on me then that until I figured out how to play this new cancer game, I needed to stop taking in liquid and nutrition by mouth. It was all just causing me too much trouble.

Now a halfway sane person, at that point, would realize, *If I don't take in liquid and nutrition by mouth, then I had better call my doc and find out how else do I keep myself from starving and dying of thirst.* No one can just stop eating and drinking and think they are going to do anything but seriously damage themselves.

But the question of reaching out and asking for help never entered my mind. The old crazy warriors had snuck out of their box and were in total control. What I did—without any conscious thought or decision—was get tough, hunker down, "ride it out," and just fight it through. So for over a week I didn't take in enough sustenance to keep a worm alive. To say the least, I spiraled down pretty fast.

The day of my meeting, 12/2/2010, was by far the worst day of my cancer experience. When Paula was driving me to the appointment, I told her that I felt like opening the door of the car, rolling out, and hoping to hell whatever was behind us was big enough to finish the job. It was bad.

What I desperately wanted to do was ambush the meeting, tell my good doctor from the very start that I didn't care what the CT scan said or where my cancer was. What I wanted to do was close my eyes, fall on the floor, pass out, and not wake up until it was safe. And if it was never safe, then I never wanted to be conscious in this world again.

But ambushing meetings is not my style. I wait my turn. I so badly wanted help but didn't know if I could or had the right to make my needs the top priority. I was struggling about what to do. Then a most wonderful and not-so-strange thing happened, at least not strange to me. I've been there too many times for it to be strange.

God co-opts people. He moves in and takes them over. Both are present, yet clearly it is God doing the business. I've thought of this as Michelangelo and his brushes. No one sanctifies Michelangelo's brushes. The brush does not make the masterpiece—only the Master makes the masterpiece. Yet without the brushes, the wall would remain bare. And without the "touch of the Master's hand," brushes are just poor, impotent things.

Like I said, I've been co-opted too many times to ever

doubt that such divine things happen. And it did then, for me.

My dad showed himself to me in my struggle, and the power of Father flowing through him shone like the sun. The terrible black power was gone. All that came through my dad, as the one blood of the True Vine, was a life full of Father's love that was now also flowing through my dad.

He looked me in the face like he never had (although I knew he had always loved me with all his soul), put his loving hands on my shoulders, and said in a way that went to the level of my struggle, "The war is over. You aren't alone. Jump to the front of the line. Ask for what you need." Then he gave me a wink and said, "Don't worry. We'll see that you get what you need. We've got you in our arms. We have you covered." And, of course, I knew that the "we" he was talking about was he and the Master.

I asked Paula to attach an account of this divine co-opting from an old God File about Trish in Australia. I ask you to read it if you want. God is at the end of our noses. If it takes a little co-opting to break through the rock that binds our hearts, then He surely will—and does.

I think this co-opting experience happens a lot to people,

but we never find the forum to share these marvelous examples of God's passionate goodness toward us. Or are embarrassed? All of which minimizes the miracle.

When God takes over inside us, we become the brush as the Master sets to work leading us back home. Have you ever experienced being taken over by the Master? Have you ever told anyone about it? If not, why not?

From the God File:

It's Okay, Trish

I was several stages past exhausted and had been for days. This was my last talk of this Australian swing. I was done in to the point of hearing voices and being, once again, nothing but a walking, empty, aching shell. I was done, but God wasn't.

I had just finished the all-afternoon seminar at a large hospital that also offered mental health services as well as a wide range of treatment options, including detox, a methadone program, and a full inpatient and outpatient chemical dependency program. By the end of the session, "I" had retreated inside, seeking some safe place to hide while my mouth and body went through the motions of delivering my seminar. Every part of me ached and begged to go find a quiet, dark place to hide in.

After I'd talked to the dozen or so people who came up as I was edging toward the door, an older man approached. His face was deeply lined, his hair white, his manner almost timid—like he was afraid to say whatever motivated him to come forward.

He told me he worked at the detox downstairs and wondered if I would mind stopping by the unit to meet the residents, since "We use your videos all the time. It would give them a lift if you would greet them."

A slight buzzing started in the back of my brain. I've experienced this sensation a million times. Right or wrong, I've come to understand it as a kind of wake-up call from God. The buzzing tells me there is something important about to take place. To me, it is God saying, "Wake up. Pay attention. I have some work for you to do."

When this buzzing starts, the same thing always happens. No matter how tired or hurt or distracted I may be, I am jerked awake and aware at that moment. It feels like being in a totally dark room and suddenly a powerful flashbulb goes off in my face. Instant overload. Only it isn't really overload; it is more like a sense of being possessed or taken over. Some consciousness or awareness I choose to call God fills me and dispels any other consideration but focusing entirely on the business He has in mind.

I find it impossible to not follow the invitation when the buzzing starts. During this time or this "state," I have been removed. Another has taken up residence inside me.

This detox was a locked unit. Immediately inside the locked door stood three or four of the residents. All were under thirty and did indeed seem amazed that "the guy from the films" came to see them. One of these residents was special. She stood out—she had a halo of light around her head.

This woman's name was Trish. Her eyes were shining and she was hugely excited, hopping around like a child in need of a bathroom break. Trish was painfully thin. I thought she was perhaps anorexic as well as an addict. She said she was Persian, and her complexion was like cream-colored coffee. Her jeans were well worn and had stars stitched on them. She wore a sleeveless denim vest with a motorcycle club's colors sewn to the back. I think she probably liked the biker boys.

God had painted a bull's-eye on her back as well. I heard Him say in His wordless way, "This is important, so pay attention. Here we go."

Trish was so nervous, she didn't have words

to express her excitement. She danced around sputtering a word or two, then just stopped and looked at me with those sparkling eyes. "I've relapsed a thousand times," she said. "I've put everything there is in my veins, up my nose, and down my throat. But I think I can make it this time." The buzzing filled my head. It dawned on me with crystal clarity that she was the main rea-son—at least that I was aware of—why I was called to come all the way to Australia.

God had dressed me in the costume of the "man in the movies" because that gave Him ac-cess to His daughter's depth. He told me to use the costume, act the part He put me in. If my being in the film meant something to Trish, then so be it. Good, God could use that. I told Trish to get something to write on. I wanted to leave her something signed.

"Really?" she said and disappeared down the cluttered hallway that countless feet had walked, Lazarus-like, as they returned from the dead. She came back with one of the flyers they had around the hospital advertising my seminar. I watched my hand write, "To a beautiful woman who is my friend. I count on your prayers."

I know "I watched my hand write" sounds strange. Why not simply say, "I wrote"? Again, the reason is because in this state, I am just an observer. I'm no more than a glove covering a hand. The hand does what it wants—the glove simply goes along for the ride. Even as the words appeared on Trish's flyer, I thought, *Wow. That seems like an overly familiar thing to write to a woman you just met.* But then the thought came to me like someone whispering an aside to someone in a movie or play: *You have just met her. I've known Trish from the beginning.*

So I just sat back and waited to see what God had in mind for my body and mind to do.

I asked her to read back to me what I wrote. She couldn't. Not because she was illiterate, but because the words saying she was a beautiful woman and that someone considered her a friend and counted on her prayers were beyond her comprehension. In her mind, such things had nothing to do with her world. The words might as well have been written in Martian.

With perfect clarity—because what was going on was not from or about me—the Presence in me asked her to repeat after me the words I had written. I spoke what the Presence had written, a single word at a time, and she slowly, almost painfully, repeated them after me. As she re-peated the words telling of her worth and beauty, it seemed the ground on some level shook. The stone was rolled away, and Lazarus came blinking from the dark into the light of a new day.

Ten or so minutes later, I got ready to leave. "As it happened," the man who was driving me around had already left to get the car. I asked Trish to walk with me to the locked door of the unit. We had a moment before the door was electronically opened. The buzz was fully in control. I gave her a big hug, which was more than a little surprising to her, I think. She was scared. She was just a bag of bones. I held her, but she was not able to hug me back.

I heard myself say into her ear, "It's okay, Trish. Grab ahold. God wants you to know there is always someone bigger than you watching over you." Slowly, I felt her arms close around my back until she was not just hugging but hanging on for all she was worth.

That's all. The message was delivered. Seconds later, the door opened. I left, exchanging with her the pledge that we would pray for each other every day so neither one of us would have to go forward alone.

It probably took me another fifteen seconds to walk to the car, get in, and ride away. In those seconds, the buzz left and my exhausted, numb state returned. What mattered, though, was not how I felt but whether the message got delivered or not. I've encountered this process a million times. When I stop to think about it, it seems strange that such things happen. Do they for everyone? I guess it doesn't matter. However such things might be for someone else is no business of mine. It is how it is for me in the tiny patch of the garden given to me. That's all I need to know.

• • •

P.S. Almost a year has passed since I met Trish. I got this email from friends in Australia this morning. "Trish from Herbert Clinic (the lady whom you said you would pray for and whom you asked to pray for you) died last week. She overdosed after going out once again with a male partner who had an investment in her not getting clean. Lydia (her primary counselor) and John (her secondary counselor) both wanted me to tell you that after your visit, she definitely improved and was much brighter. They said she had had a history of abusive partners. God rest her soul, and may she now have peace. Lydia and John both appeared tender about the relationship you formed ever so briefly with her."

I cried as I read this, but there was also a flood of light behind the tears. I realized, God can be a biker boy. I had heard His big motorcycle come roaring around the corner in Trish's last moments as He came to fetch her home. I saw her get up whole and clean, light streaming from her face, as one's face always gets when in the presence of a lover. I saw her climb up behind her giant hero, grab hold of Him who was the one she always longed to grab onto anyway. He smiled at her, looking over His shoulder. It was the smile of one who knows, saying to her, "Enough of this, Trish. Enough! It's time to leave. We'll point this old hog into the sun and ride forever. I got you now, and I'll never drop you or leave you alone." Then I heard the big cycle give a throaty roar like a million lions, and off they went. Just the two of them, heading into the sun, beyond any power that could ever again halt their journey.

* * *

Now, back to my meeting with my oncologist. So I did ambush the meeting. I told the doctor everything I put here. He looked at Paula and our daughter Erin, who went with us, to see if they validated my story or if I was suffering some form of cancer-caused insanity. They told him if I was saying it, then that is what I felt.

The doctor immediately took me back to the infusion room, where I was given a saline drip with some steroids (for "pop" he said) and antinausea medicine. The nurse had trouble finding a vein to put the needle in. She said, "You are terribly dehydrated. Every time I touch a vein, it collapses. You're lucky you got here when you did."

But she got the drip going. Within a half hour, I was feeling much better. My spirit was coming back with the fluid. I was moving back into the best A.C. existence. (B.C. is before cancer. A.C. is after cancer.) The next day, I went in and had another double-boost infusion of my saline concoction. They will be at least weekly now.

Later we had our meeting with my doc. My cancer has progressed faster than any of us had expected. There are a few minor treatment options we might try, but since I am Stage IV and "beyond anything modern medicine can do for you," the doc said his best guess is my time is about three months. I pushed it to between three and six months, but all of it is a guess. No one knows but the Master. There is certainly a power beyond medical science.

The great, good blessing in my case is that I am amazingly pain free. That allows me to put protocols like acupuncture, meditation, breathing, and spending a lot of time with my clan both on this side of the veil and the other. I listen to a lot of Christmas music. Learning how to best live with my cancer has a steep learning curve. But I'm learning. I feel as good as I ever have A.C.

The trick from here on out, no matter how many days or months I have, is to erase "have to" from my slate and only do what gives me peace, hope, love, and meaning. That's what I am doing as best I can. A major task is to keep in the context of "I have cancer," slow down, and only do what I have the strength to do. This is now. This is not before.

Since there is a bit of a change in the timelines mentioned, I thought it might keep more to our storyline by starting "Letters part 2." More like, Okay, I better understand the new game. So how do I best play out the days and time I have? So that's what part 2 is. It will have lessons rather than rounds. Dancing lessons, in fact.

———

{PAULA} Earnie and I sure talked about the "Trish" experience. I also happened to be there and could see what was taking place. It was obvious to both of us that she was the real reason we were at the treatment center at the hospital. Dr. Stephen Jurd, a psychiatrist, had set up the training for his staff. We had met him at the first Australian conference, the one where we began the connection to the Sally. He is from Sydney and said he would be happy to be our tour guide when we came to visit. He and his wife, Libby, did indeed become our unofficial tour guides whenever we went to Australia. Asking for help and allowing others to give us their help have been big lessons for Earnie; but that was what the cancer time did—it was his turn to feel what it is like when God carries us.

At the beginning of December every year, I have all of the women from my Saturday morning support group over for a holiday dinner. I put out all the good dishes, iron the napkins, and make the food. Our two daughters, Erin and Cara, and now our oldest granddaughter, Ella, help serve the meal. My Sacred Sisters are a great support to me and they so loved Earnie. After Earnie and I did the Life Management Program with them a few years ago, some of us formed accountability groups. The program is about how to find "The Lie" in your life. Then, once you find it, the new practice of changing that "lie" begins; this is where the accountability group comes in.

Most in our group (which is now over twenty years old) were able to come this year. In previous years, Earnie would go out earlier in the evening and then come back to see the women before they went home, but this night he was here when they arrived. It gave many of the women an opportunity to connect with him, even if it was just for a short time. I remember that one of the women, Juana— who was American Indian and Mexican—was wearing a beaded hummingbird ornament that her sister had made.

Earnie commented about how lovely it was—and sure enough, soon it was hanging up for him to see every day near all the angels in our living-room window.

After we said the prayer before dinner, Earnie had a few words to share. He talked about how important it was to express to others that you love them—and then to accept when they tell you that they love you as well. It was what Earnie has felt for years, but the receiving part was new. This was also something new for Ella. Right after he finished his message, Ella came up to Earnie and said, "I so love you, Grandpa," and he replied, "I so love you, Ella." She had many tears, but the two of them just hung on to each other and supported each other. It was such a lovely scene to witness. Although she was sad, Ella had had the courage to get out her words, and Earnie absorbed her message. He told me later it felt so good for him to hear her laugh as the night went on.

. . .

Lessons

I know the transition to get to this second part of my journey, as I describe it here, has been jerky. I apologize for that. I don't know how to change it. But I want to move past the "maybe three months left" moment in the doctor's office. That was then. The journey was then. But this is now. My journey has taken a different (and to me wonderful) turn. I want you to go with me past the "three months" into this new place.

The letters in part 1 were about "rounds." Notice the letters from this new place are about lessons. There is a difference. What we are talking about now is learning to

Dance with God

(I wish I had a way to put those words, "DANCE WITH GOD," in color or italics or bursting flames.) I hope you get what I am trying to say.

The Dance

December 2010

God rose up and said as clearly as the moon speaks to the tides, "I have danced with you every day of your life. What is left is for you to dance with me."

Learning this dance takes countless forms. Here is one of them: Many of you, my family, expressed real distress at the "three months left" news. That was my good doctor's best educated guess at the time, given the facts in front of him. That is his guess. It's not mine. All anyone has is a guess. And since the cancer is in my body, I figure my guess comes first.

As I learn to let myself dance with my God, to keep focused on Him, things have changed a lot since last week. As I learn to open my heart to all the incredible love coming from you, my family, I feel strength pouring into me. My core is strengthening. I see and feel my God smile at me— sometimes He even winks—and say, "See, I told you. Trust me. We are on a wonderful journey."

Your love astounds me! It pours in from everywhere. It lifts up my body and spirit and makes them soar like an eagle—even my poor, old body. I've lost about fifty pounds to the meat grinder. I look like an emaciated, pot-bellied stork. (Pot-bellied because of all the fluid build-up in my abdominal cavity.) All my life I have gladly jumped into the pit and fought to the death in the name of God for others' spiritual freedom. I've fought the red mist in the lives of others forever—and seen the miracles. I've seen the power that only "I love you" possesses at its fiery core to create transformed lives (which is dancing with God).

But now that same "in the pit" do-or-die commitment is coming back to me from you. Now it is pouring into me. And with that, God winks and says, "It is your time. Let us enjoy this together."

I need you all to know the last thing in the world I am doing is lying in bed waiting for sweet Jesus to take me around the bend. Maybe that will happen at the end when I'm forced to take pain-numbing medications. But that isn't now.

If something comes in the door trying to kill me or any of my family, I am compelled to run at it and do everything I can to kill it first. And by that I do not mean a few swings, but if the fight gets too tough I'll take leave to heal, retreat, and try again another day.

No, no. What I mean is *to the death*. I mean, I burned my boat on the beach. There is no retreat. I mean that fine madness that gladly jumps in the pit with the savage beast knowing you can't be beat because you don't fear dying.

I forced this point last Friday pretty hard with my guys at the Sally. I told them, "I am going to finish my race strong!" I am going in honor of and in the company of my all-good God, who never did anything but good to me; not that it was always easy. But my God hung on the cross with me year after year. The beast was after me, but He always kept by my side. Often He got right on that cross with me. He kept telling me that I needed to learn what the cross had to teach me, but that He would always lead me to a better place. And He did. I am at one of those far better places now.

I told the guys that they knew exactly what I was talking about. Call the beast cancer or addiction—and always the spiritual sickness under addiction. The name of what is trying to kill us doesn't matter. What matters is the howl that comes in the dark hours screaming into our body and nervous system, "You can't do this. You are beyond hope. You are beyond forgiveness. You have been to prison too many times. You have hurt too many people. Don't be a fool! No one will ever love you. You aren't worth it. You are a loser, a victim. You are beyond help."

If we haven't burned our ship on the shore, if we aren't willing to fight to the death, then death will take us away, like it has everyone in that room—or we wouldn't be back in treatment again. These guys all know what fighting for their lives means.

Yes, I told the guys I was going to finish strong, but not without them. I needed them to make the same kind of commitment to me as I made to them. I went eye to eye with the beast for them a thousand times. Now I need them to do the same for me. I need to grab ahold of them in the wee, desperate hours when the enemy is on me. I need them to hold me up in the name of the God who holds us all up. And we'd end up laughing at death because, deeply connected down to the level of total commitment, death has no power over us.

As is true of my family at the Sally, so it is true of you, my family everywhere.

So in addition to my twice-weekly saline drips (as well as pursuing other aids from the past, such as EMDR [Eye Movement Desensitization and Reprocessing], hypnotherapy, nutritional counseling, breathing work, endless talk therapy, meditation, and near-constant visualization), I have added acupuncture and massage in the last ten or so days. I'm doing everything I can to kick my cancer's ass.

But in truth my fight is not against cancer. Cancer isn't my enemy. The real enemies are all the "old lies" that try to poison my response to cancer.

Love makes my total commitment to life rather than death possible. *You* make it possible.

Let me tell you one small example of this healing power of being "up and doing." It makes me laugh. I call it my "in-house Olympics."

My spirit, supported by your love, tells me, "The longer you lie around, the weaker you will get." Our house is a split-level. There are six steps from the bottom floor to the landing, then eight steps from the landing to the top floor. My spirit said to climb those steps three or four extra times a day. Move your muscles. Get better.

I laugh picturing this skinny, sick old man going up and down those steps in the plodding, sluggish way that A.C. (after cancer) allows. It makes me think of our long jumper in round 8 who couldn't get from the takeoff board to the pit. But those are my Olympics, and if it helps, then I am going to be hard at it.

So know this, we are up and doing. My dance partner tells me, "Attaboy. We'll run this string out as far as you are meant to go—and laugh all the way to the finish line."

It's all good and *really cool.*

I love you all.

Onward,
Earnie

———

{PAULA} Earnie felt it important to show the guys at the Sally that although his body was weak, his spirit was strong. He did show them what was going on by holding up his arms, which were very thin by this time. He felt they needed to see this. It is only the body that was weak and worn out.

"*I am going to finish strong*" were vital words to him. We again made our commitment to each other and went onward together!

• • •

Lesson 2

The Heartbeat of the Dance

December 2010

It's about 2 a.m. I'm rolling around the house in my fast-becoming-nightly routine. Not all bad. I like the quiet and got several good naps in earlier. The house—both my inner and outer house—is packed so full of the joyful, silent swoosh of angels' wings that I am lost in the wonder of it all. Truly amazed, lost, and knocked over.

We had a party earlier at my regular Friday night Salvation Army class. It's been several weeks since I've been able to attend. The party was all about the merging of two crystal streams, charged with grace and grit. That is, me seeing my guys and they me.

I've sat here in a kind of daze looking at the computer screen for about twenty minutes now. I raise my hand to tap keys to start sharing with you even the slightest slice of what happened. What happened were the stories, of course. God lives in the stories. All of life's stories are little maps of how God so passionately seeks to dance with us.

The daze is because it is too much: the stories too overwhelming, too rich, too powerful. No book or pen by the greatest writers in the world (for some reason I am thinking of the characters Damon Runyon created) could match my guys. The characters bowl me over. I can't even start to tell you.

I'm afraid to say a single name. If I did, it would be like a leak springing from a dam. Pretty soon the leak would become a torrent, and the dam would collapse. It's so hard not to mention a single name. But I don't dare.

I believe I've told you of the strings of blue lights my dear Paula has spread across the deck out back. It snowed recently, and that snow has created snow domes over each light. Now as I look out, I see dozens and dozens of individual blue lights glowing inside their houses of snow. It's beautiful.

What the sight seems to represent to my spirit are these great characters. Each dome a character from earlier. Each light in those domes a totally unique, totally powerful, totally beautiful merging of our crystal streams. I can, of course, no more explain or even describe all this any more than I could the actual earlier events.

So I am just going to sit here a while longer, looking at the lights, and say, "Thank you, God." And just let you know that this house is full of angels' wings beating out the heartbeat of the dance.

Cancer is nothing. Love is all.

Onward,
Earnie

*   *   *

{PAULA} Following is an entry from Earnie's God File that seems fitting to share here:

The Humble Cathedral

The stage was beautiful. The singers were some of the world's best. The auditorium was packed. Special lighting seemed to create a whole new atmosphere of otherworldly peace and serenity. Mostly it seemed they sang spiritual songs, not necessarily traditional hymns but songs praising God and various aspects of living a spiritual life. Every time they finished a song, the crowed clapped and clapped. They were instantly rewarded with overwhelming applause and love. Their songs created a cathedral where the Spirit ruled supreme.

Cathedrals are always awe-inspiring. Their purpose is to fill the human spirit with a realization of the greatness of God as compared to our own tiny reality.

I was in a cathedral this morning. Yet it was a humble thing. There were no great walls or precious works of art in stone and paint. This cathedral was just an old, shabby room with cigarette-scarred tables. Ten of us men were there. We were tiny. We all are tiny. Yet as the men began to share their stories of transformation through grace, it seemed to me that, just like the staging on the TV program, lights came on, souls rose up to the face of God, and grace so thoroughly embraced the space that there was no air to breathe but that of the living God coming to rescue His lost sons.

Our group is called God's Junkyard Dogs. Junkyard Dogs because we need to fight with tooth and claw and stand firm in our decision to live a spiritual life in situations that would be totally impossible to maintain without the sustaining Spirit of God.

The transformation of the lives of these worthy men is grander and gives more glory to God than a thousand cathedrals filled with silver and gold, because in our humble cathedral there is nothing material to protect or hide away; nothing gets in the way of our purpose: to support one another with all our power to live up to our purpose and worth. This worth is determined only by the heart of God. As a large prison tattoo of one of the men inked on a huge bicep read, "Judged only by God."

One man spoke of the time he pulled his pistol and robbed the dope man. Another told of not having a change of clothes or a cent for food as he limped down the street ailing from a bullet wound in his leg. Yet another told of being "tricked" by the pastor telling him the treatment program was only six weeks long, when in fact it turned out to be six months. Other men had been tricked in the same way. But now they sit at the altar of our cathedral, hearts and lives cracked open to the light of God's grace. Now they speak of power rather than wielding force on the street. They are changed men. A saint named Anselm has this quote attributed to him: "The glory of God is man fully alive." Or was it, "Nowhere does God come closer to man than in man"? Whenever those lines were said and whoever said them, their perfect fulfillment was right there, in us and among us, vibrating with grace within the spiritual walls of our humble cathedral.

As much as any human being is capable of knowing the mind of God, I felt with complete certainty that our Father was proud of us. I am certain He looked down on our humble gathering and whispered in everyone's soul, as He did mine, "I'm proud of you. Just keep on coming down the road. I am with you every step of the way."

Our cathedral is a thing of beauty, outshined by none, where lives the glory of God.

———

{PAULA} Jerry Junkman, a counselor from the Sally, set up a pizza party for Earnie after the Friday night class. This gave the men an opportunity to have a little visit with Earnie. Many are now a part of the "Junkyard Dogs."

Earnie loved blue Christmas lights and had since the first time we saw them, so this year I was in search of blue outdoor lights for him. I had all of our family members and many friends searching as well. Then a dear lady who cuts my hair, Carolyn, said, "My husband says if you need something, go to Menards." So off I went, and there they were. Montgomery and I put up the blue lights on the deck railing and around the tree in front of our house.

Now, here is a little side note: Every year at the beginning of December, St. Catherine University (where I went to college) has vespers. My daughters and I try to attend, and this is the official beginning of the holiday season for us. It is such a peaceful way to begin this very busy season. There are two places that I hold as "sacred places" in my heart: one is the gym of St. Joan of Arc Church here in

Minneapolis, and the other is Our Lady of Victory Chapel at St. Kate's in St. Paul. I feel so at peace when I enter those places.

Sure enough, as I drove up to St. Kate's (another name for St. Catherine University) this year, there were two huge evergreen trees decorated in those wonderful, vibrant blue lights. God is good! About a week later I loaded Earnie in the car one night and we drove over to St. Kate's just so he could see the blue lights. A dear time for both of us!

. . .

Lesson 3

We Must Learn Self-Compassion

December 2010

Just had my massage and acupuncture sessions. I have them every week. They seem to help, so why not? The lesson is to grow enough self-compassion that we are willing to go proactive and try whatever might help. If a vicious enemy comes into your yard, what else is there to do but pick up every weapon you can lay hand to and have at that enemy? We must learn to care about ourselves, yes?

I thought of a great "last gesture." When I finally pass, I hope someone props up my corpse, puts a shotgun sideways to my great bloated belly, and blows the poisonous liquid inside it to hell. What a great picture. I think it says it all pretty well.

Acceptance is often at the head of the self-compassion list. There is no moving through getting gutted in life without total acceptance. That is, acceptance without resentment and the need to somehow "get even" or "make them pay." "They" won't pay; we will.

The picture of my sister Carol standing at the grave of her dearly beloved son Rich comes to mind. Carol's husband Dick was a super athlete—tall and handsome. Carol was and is smart. She could always get any grade she wanted in any class she ever took. So her assumption was her son, her first child, would be this tall, smart, blessed child. What could be better than that?

What she got was this perfectly formed but small child—but a child who had the absolute genius of getting to what was real. He immediately and naturally saw to the core of things. Carol said it was at an Al-Anon meeting that a great truth hit her: who and what Rich was, wasn't better than the tall, smart son; it was better than she could have imagined. God is always about "better" if we keep our eyes halfway open.

Let me tell you a bit of Rich's genius and something of his passing:

1. At one point, Rich was an orderly at a hospital. One person in his care was an old man whose greatest time seemed to be when he played football for Wisconsin. He was a Badger through and through.

Rich was on hand for this man's last moments. Without thought or decision, because it was just who he was, Rich moved as close to the old man as he could and whispered into his ear, "Once a Badger, always a Badger." And on those golden words, the old man turned young again and raced away over his beloved gridiron.

That was Rich's genius: always and immediately get to the core of what counted.

2. With every death in a private home—Rich died in the room next to his mom—the coroner must be involved. Carol said the coroner took one look at Rich's face and said, "Well, no foul play here. Look at the joyful look on his face. This man went to someone he loved."

We reap what we sow. I think Rich saw his beloved grandfather come to get him. I think little Odin saw big Odin come for him and was more than happy to leap onto the dragon ship, and off they went.

3. That's what Carol said. She knew in her heart, he was just "fetched." It was his time and he was fetched home.

Rich died. Crushed, defeated, broken, wounded to the core, Carol stood at her champion warrior's grave. Total acceptance, she said, was her only way out. Of course her life would never be the same. Life never is after such a tragedy. *"But,"* she said, "it can't be all. My loss can't be everything." She said she had to learn a way to live that made room for life while always keeping in her heart a chapel, so to speak, where Rich lived and she could visit whenever she needed to.

Every brokenhearted person in the world understands these words.

Without acceptance, our hearts are forever blocked. Blocked hearts are sick hearts. No one lives well if a mountain of petrified tears are hiding in the dark. Breaking out, bursting through the eggshell that holds us captive is the only way to gain freedom. And that takes acceptance. Acceptance is the ticket into the dance.

Onward,
Earnie

———

{PAULA} Acceptance was the "ticket into the dance"—somehow acceptance was always part of this picture, and we both knew it. I am very grateful for this gift. I am even more grateful today that the time we had wasn't wasted on not accepting what was to be. It really is true that the little things in life make all the difference.

So I let the tears come when they may, which still surprises me. Not that they come—that is expected—but when they come. I feel his presence around me right now as I work on this manuscript. Who would have thought how healing all this writing would be for me? Certainly not me.

Lesson 4

A Voice from Somewhere

December 2010

Monte, my oldest grandson and bodyguard, aka Big Butch, and I were visiting Big Mike where he lives. We'd been hanging out a while when Big Mike looks through the glass window, sees someone, and starts frantically waving them in. "You got to meet this guy; Shorty is special."

So in comes this small man, brimming with energy. He seemed to bounce as he walked, with his head tilted up. Of course, I was sitting down and so I couldn't see his eyes—he seemed to always be looking up.

When Mike said, "This is my best friend Earnie," Shorty quickly came over to me. Shorty said he first met me through one of our films while he was in prison. But he said he knew Mike and I were tight, so that said everything.

We all talked a bit about recovery. Shorty has been clean and sober fifteen years. I asked him how that happened for him. He said the last time he was released from prison, he was headed right back to his crack place. He had relapsed there many times.

"So what happened when you got it?" I asked. The story was really heating up. As I said, I couldn't see his eyes but I could see enough to know they were getting wet. He said, "A voice from somewhere told me, 'Not this time.'" It was time to quit. So he did. He's been free since that moment when the voice from somewhere talked to him.

We, you and I, know whose voice it is and where it comes from. It's the great God telling us to go tell someone He wants to dance with them. It's God calling our name, telling us "and I want to dance with you."

It's all there if only we learn to listen.

As Monte and I were getting ready to leave, Mike asked me to bless him. He told me that in the Bible when Elijah was being taken to heaven, he blessed the prophet coming along behind him. He passed his spirit to the next chosen one.

Mike, this good, holy, God-embraced man, wanted me to bless him, to pass my spirit on to him. He was deadly, passionately serious. Tears were in his eyes. He took his cap off, leaned in real close, and said, "Please pass on your blessing to me."

So like two prophets standing on an ancient hill surrounded by mystery and the fire of God, we did the best I could. This was all new to me. But I put my hand on his bowed old head and poured every ounce of love and sense of my God dancing with me into this redeemed warrior. It was a sacred moment. I don't know if Big Butch got a picture of this moment or not. I hope so. God's face doesn't always emerge through the veil so clearly. Oh my, such a moment!

Later, wee hours, 3:45 a.m.

I just woke up from a bit of a dream, I guess. Father often uses dreams. This one had imagery from a lot of recent moments.

In the dream I was in a crowd with Shorty and Mike and my two daughters' families, and Trish (our friend from Australia) was there as well. I was wearing one of my prayer shawls around my neck. The folks who do my massage and acupuncture milled about. My pastor, Reverend Hunter, and the first lady, Brenda, from my church were moving around, laughing and praying at the same time. My mom and dad showed up. All kinds of other people on this journey with me were all moving around dancing with God. . . . (Like you.)

On the fringe of the crowd, a young man was watching all of this. He stood in the shadows for a while, but then he stepped up. He reached through a hole of some kind, through all the activity that swirled around me. This reaching through a hole was very clear to me.

Reaching through the hole, he touched me. It was magic. The touch said, "See, we are dancing. We are fine. I have you and won't let go. When it's time, I'll hold you tight and we'll sail through all this red mist with ease. But that's for then. For now, let's just keep dancing."

Later still.

I need to share this with you. Several nights ago, I was in bad shape. My PTSD was roaring like a hundred enraged, starving lions. They were out to kill me. It was about 3 a.m. My stomach from hell was full of gas and poison. It was killing me. Pain was rolling around in me like the ball in a pinball machine, everything lit up. I was driven to my knees—literally.

I found myself lying on the bathroom floor, with no idea if I could get up or not. My head was in the toilet. What little protein drink I had taken in the day was barfed right there in front of me. My sides ached from throwing it up. I wanted to quit.

From that wasteland, all I could do was throw out a single word: "Help." Then the most incredible thing happened, incredible and literal! I mean, this happened. My big brother Jesus was immediately there.

What He did was *climb right on top of me on my cross.* He covered me. His face was right on mine. *He came to protect me.* He looked me in the face. I knew He was holding the soft-bodied little thing I was. He kept telling me it was okay. He had me. He held me. He asked me to believe and accept there was a reason why my head was in the toilet. I didn't need to know what that reason was. I just needed to accept that it was so.

There is nothing quick, I don't think, about hanging on one's cross. We hang until we don't anymore. Sooner or later everything passes, even the cross. Then another truly amazing thing happened.

As I looked at my Savior, I saw the faintest glimmer of a smile on His face. He kept looking at me. I started to smile too. Then I got it. Jesus started to laugh, and so did I. Even with my head still in the toilet, I started to laugh. "Good," said the Spartan. "Then at least we will fight in the shade."

We were laughing because, whether on the cross right then or not, I wasn't going to stay on that cross. Death had no claim on us. I knew I would get up somehow. This terrible night would pass. Others might come later—and probably would—but those would pass as well. We'd laugh at death all over again.

All of this was (and is) truly profound to me. The suffering was real, but so was the *incredible experience* of my

Savior covering me on my cross. "I got you," He said. "We'll come through this. I'll protect you as my own, because you are."

I'm out of words, as there are no words for me to express the wonder of the experience of God being willing to cover me on my cross.

I finally got out of the bathroom by crawling on my hands and knees to a chair in the outer room. I don't know how long it took me to elbow and haul my bony butt into the chair. But I made it. I rested there awhile until I was finally able to stand up. From there I guess I found I could move. Not pretty, but then cancer isn't pretty. Still, nothing beats knowing, covered by the King, I can flip cancer the bird and keep on trucking.

Even later.

I want to close this lesson with a bit from one of my favorite poems, "Renascence." The poet is Edna St. Vincent Millay. Her poem is about a man who got down so low, he wished he were dead. So he got what he wanted. He sunk down into his own grave. After a while, he didn't think that was such a great choice. He missed being alive (dancing with God), so he prayed he might live again. Because God never gives up on us, sure enough, a great whoosh of light and grace brought him out of his grave.

The last part of the poem I want to share with you is who he was when he woke up. It goes like this:

Ah! Up then from the ground sprang I
And hailed the earth with such a cry
As is not heard save from a man
Who has been dead, and lives again.

About the trees my arms I wound;
Like one gone mad I hugged the ground;
I raised my quivering arms on high;
I laughed and laughed into the sky,
Till at my throat a strangling sob
Caught fiercely, and a great heart-throb
Sent instant tears into my eyes;
Oh God, I cried, no dark disguise
Can e'er hereafter hide from me
Thy radiant identity!
Thou canst not move across the grass
But my quick eyes will see Thee pass,
Nor speak, however silently,
But my hushed voice will answer Thee.
I know the path that tells Thy way
Through the cool eve of every day;
God, I can push the grass apart
And lay my finger on Thy heart!

The world stands out on either side
No wider than the heart is wide;
Above the world is stretched the sky, —
No higher than the soul is high.
The heart can push the sea and land
Farther away on either hand;
The soul can split the sky in two,
And let the face of God shine through.
But East and West will pinch the heart
That can not keep them pushed apart;
And he whose soul is flat—the sky
Will cave in on him by and by.

Okay, poem is over. Seems to me she is saying we either learn to dance with God or our souls die.

It's all pretty cool.

Onward,
Earnie

———

{PAULA} He loved the time when he, Mike, and Montgomery were together. Earnie was always able to see Mike's true gifts—a leader. We are all called and, if we listen, we will hear what that calling is.

As long as I have known Earnie, he loved the poetry book *One Hundred and One Famous Poems*. It was his favorite. His dear sister Carol gave this book to him in 1988 when he had lost his 1959 copy—so you see, he had loved this poem for many years. Earnie was always reading and learning. He had so many interests and loved seeing how principles fit together in life. If a principle is true in one area, then it was true in another area.

I, too, learned a valuable lesson here. If I asked for help for us, I got nothing, nada, not a lick of help. But when I asked for help for me, it came immediately. How can this be? What is this about? It took me some time to figure this out, but during those days it seemed like I needed a lot of help and often. Eventually, I did figure it out. My lesson, it seemed to me, was to ask for help for myself—make it a personal request.

• • •

Lesson 5

When the Egg Breaks

December 2010

Dear James,

Fifteen or so years ago when I started emerging from behind the "old lie," I felt like an egg was breaking and I was coming out. I was like a lot of guys in our group now. Learning to live through our hearts, rather than our heads, is different! It's scary. But our chance is here.

It is important to me that the special men in my group have a piece of me: Abe, a lion. Michael T., a necklace. Dockmo, a picture. All these things were mine for a long time. That's why I want to pass them along to you all.

As I was doing my work fifteen years ago, a friend got me this beautiful crystal egg. She said it was in honor of my emerging. I want you to have it. Hold it up to the light, James, and see all the color and power in it. I love it. Now it is yours. We are all in this together.

Love to you, my brother.
Earnie

{PAULA} Earnie never had a chance to write the "egg" topic, but he did talk with me about it. Then for some reason, I told James M. about it. He said Earnie had written him a letter about this, which is what I have included here.

Also, I was in search of something meaningful from Earnie's God Files when I came across the following entry, which was written about a month before we found out Earnie had cancer. I include it here for you to read and reflect upon:

The Bounce

The Bounce lives at the heart of life. Many things in life are important, but none more so than the Bounce.

There are a lot of ways to describe the Bounce. It's (finally) being sick and tired of being sick and tired. It's hitting bottom and starting the climb back up into life. It's rejecting The Lie in favor of the truth. It's when the benefits of living The Lie are less than what is to be gained by moving over to the truth.

As with everything that is truly important in this life, the Bounce is spiritual in nature. No logic can persuade someone to jump from The Lie to the truth. The jump cannot be forced. No one can be scared into the jump, at least not long term. There certainly are foxhole prayers, but in the long run if the Bounce is not founded on and sprung from a new, deep inner spring of spirituality, The Lie will return, stronger than ever, and beat the individual senseless.

There is hope. The Bounce is possible no matter how far back in a spiritual dark room a person may be chained—chained once again after a start toward confidence was begun but then lost.

As long as there is life, there is the possibility of an inner eye opening, a broken mind breaking through to see the truth, a dam breaking that allows untold tons of clear water to sweep into a once barred-up spirit. There is hope. There is always hope.

And those who love best, who will not tolerate the loved one to go forth vulnerable and unprotected into the battle of life, live for only one thing. And that one thing is to offer the Bounce to the loved one. Climbing out of one's hell, which was built on The Lie—and then turning around and doing battle for another sitting in a dark room all alone and exposed to the Monster trumps all else.

At the end of one's life, there are many ways to add up if that life was successful or not. There are many yardsticks of measurement. I can't imagine a more important or valid one, however, than, "How did you serve the Bounce? Who did you help out of hell? Were you willing to go into the dark to fetch a chained soul and bring them into the light of the truth? Were you willing to pay the price? Were you willing to stand firm when your efforts were rejected and despised? Did you not run away when the gift you brought them at great expense to yourself was called evil, and by extension, when you who brought the gift were called evil as well? Did you simply keep on saying, 'I love you' when they called the light you brought them darkness? Did you give when your well was empty and they withheld the gift of light back to you?"

The Bounce *is* Christ acted out in human terms. The Bounce is the only prayer that counts when someone is owned by "The Lie."

———

{PAULA} Hopefully everyone has some special friends in their lives, people who can always be counted on, for whatever reason. In the months before Earnie died, we had some of these people who lived in town over to our house. The intimacy of the visits was something to witness. Love and support are so very important to each of us as we go through our tough times.

My two sisters, of course, came for Earnie's funeral and celebration of life and then stayed with me the following week. They sat with me as I read through each of the cards and memorials. I don't know how I would have gotten through this time without them. We have gathered many times since then, just so we would stay more connected.

· · ·

Lesson 6

How It All Started

December 2010

How it all started: My spirit has been waiting for weeks to start this lesson. It feels important to me. I want to tell you how this whole journey started for me, long before I knew there was a journey.

So many things at the time seemed so random and accidental. Yet when I look back through my present spiritual eyes, it becomes apparent how each "random step" was choreographed like a ballet. Father was laying golden bricks in front of us each step of the way. All because He wants to dance with us—*every one of us, even me.*

Anyway, here is how it appears to me now, and I'm not so sure I had all that much to do with it.

1. What I mean by I had little to do with it is this: Who we start out to be has much to do with the genetic package we inherit in our minds, bodies, and nervous systems. We have no choice about what comes down to us. There is a part of our foundation that is just who we are and will never change.

Those genetic instructions stretch back hundreds of years. Or thousands of years, depending on how far one might want to travel back down the corridor of their own history. This is true with me and the berserkers who live in my blood.

Berserkers were the elite—or at least unique—Viking warriors. When the Viking's long ships slipped out of the dark fjords in the seventh through tenth centuries to ravage Europe and beyond, the berserkers were often the first over the side of the ship to lead the charge against the enemy they called the Skraelings.

When "the spirit was on them" and it was time to do battle, they fearlessly charged their enemy. They went in as men possessed, and, indeed, in their place and time, they were.

I've gone back through the centuries and talked with those ancestors of mine. I sat at the campfire with them. They talked with me and I with them. I needed to learn who they were so I could understand a bit more of who I am.

Who can't catch a glimpse of that wild, berserk man charging into whatever burning house God sent me? Who can't see that "when the spirit is on me," I'm over the side of the ship first without thought or decision? When God says, "Go," I'm gone.

That is part of what I mean when I say I don't think I had all that much to do with how my journey started or how it has brought me to this point of learning to dance with God.

2. But how we start out is no guarantee of how we turn out. All kinds of experiences, inner work we do as well as complex factors that are so deep we'll never see or understand them, play their role. One of those primal experiences for me was going on my knees in that hospital years ago in front of the window of heroin babies and scolding God about not *doing something* about it. And Him telling me that He was doing something about it. He was going to send me to do something about it if I would agree, which I did. I knew things were going to be different from then on. I just had no idea how different. But slowly I found out.

So let me paint you this image . . .

———

{PAULA} This was the last lesson Earnie got to write. But a story that he used in many of his talks seems to fit well here:

The year was about 1968 or '69, the height of the Vietnam protests against slaughter. Outside the White House in a cold rain gathered hundreds of protestors. They sang, chanted, waved placards, held aloft (as best they could) lighted candles. At last the protest was over. Everyone went home, except one man. He stood alone in the forbidding darkness with his little candle long extinguished. A comrade hurried by and said, "It's cold, man; pack it in for tonight. Besides, you surely don't think one man standing alone can change them, do you?" The lone soldier replied, "I'm not worried about changing them. I'm here so they don't change me."

No matter how many times I heard Earnie tell this story over the years, I always loved it. "I'm here so they don't change me." And whenever I heard it, I pictured Washington, D.C., a place we both loved.

Back to the holiday at hand. On Christmas Day of 2010, our family all came over to our house. Everything took place in the living room, and it was great. When it came time to have our meal, Earnie said he wanted to do the prayer. He started off by saying, "I was looking for an analogy that all of us would understand, and what I came up with was the 'hat trick.'" Our son-in-law played hockey, his four children all play or played hockey, and Earnie and I have gone to hundreds of games through the years. Cara's family all come too to support the kids, and my sister attends their games when she comes to our house every other holiday. So we all get what the term "hat trick" signifies (three goals scored by one player in one game). Earnie said we all have had some tears and it's good to let them fall, but it is like if you have a "hat trick" and all you think about are the mistakes you made: You miss your mark. It's important not to forget about the "hat trick." Then we went around the table and each of us shared what we were grateful and/or thankful for that day. When we do family birthdays, we go around and share what we like the best about the birthday person. Earnie and I talked many times about that being the most important tradition we had.

The day after Christmas is my birthday. Last year I had a skating party with a brunch afterward; my oldest granddaughter, Ella, told me later that it was my best birthday. The day after Christmas is a hard day to have a birthday party. What I really want to do is nap. I had planned on a repeat skating party this year, but as we drew closer to the holidays and Earnie's health declined, it became obvious that we needed to just have everyone over to our place. My sister Ellen was here from Chicago and my other sister, Dorothy, and her husband, Gene, came from Appleton, Wisconsin, for the day. Dorothy brought a periwinkle blue prayer shawl, and Earnie immediately wanted it put around his shoulders. He always loved the color blue and this was a vibrant one. I still have it on my bed and it has kept me warm many a night. We all gathered in the living room and had a great visit.

Then came the preparations for the event at Hazelden.

About a year ago, we had signed Earnie up to be the main speaker out at Hazelden for Second Sunday. Second Sunday is a mini-retreat day at Hazelden's main campus in Center City for all alumni and anyone else who is interested in coming. They line up speakers for the second Sunday of the month starting in January and continuing until spring. Earnie was traditionally the first speaker of the year and had been doing the Second Sunday for many years. He so wanted to do it this year. I gave him many chances to get out of it, to get a substitute, but it was clear he wanted to do it. He always tried to bring a few people along with him, so they could share their stories too. Service work was very important to Earnie. He believed it helped everyone. It was a win-win situation.

From that point on, everything we did or didn't do was to help Earnie get ready and be able to get out to Hazelden. We rented an electric recliner chair for our living room to make it easier for Earnie to get out of the chair. We also rented a wheelchair, since Hazelden is big and walking around had become difficult for him. The Holy Spirit was so good and faithful; I'd think of these things and then start to laugh, as I knew these things were coming to me because I had asked for help. That was my big lesson to learn—ask for help. The night before the Second Sunday event, we had Montgomery stay overnight so that he could help me get Earnie into the car for the drive up to Center City. Earnie's brother Steve and his wife, Milena, also made the trip with us.

We made a handout so that if Earnie's voice gave out, the audience could still figure out what he wanted to share with them and what they were supposed to share in their small groups. He was always the educator.

After his talk, people lined up as they always did. One woman asked him to be her angel when he got to the other side, and he said yes. Women from "Boot Camp" (an alternative to jail) made him a quilt to wrap himself in, and he had that on his lap as we left Hazelden for the last time. It was a glorious day and he loved it. Also, Hazelden gave him an award that day called the Earnie Larsen Pass It On Fund. With this fund, 20 percent of all donations made to BookAid will help continue Earnie's powerful mission of helping those on the road to recovery. As he encountered and mentored those in need, he also reached out to BookAid, which would send recovery resources to help them on their path.

Although the day was good, that night was a different story. I woke about 2:30 to check on him, and he wasn't doing very well. I called the hospice nurse, and she recommended I give him some of the pain medication that had arrived the Thursday before, when we had signed up for hospice. Over the phone, she calmly walked me through the whole procedure. Afterward, he seemed to drift back to resting, if not sleeping.

On Monday, January 10, 2011, our son-in-law John came over to help me take Earnie to the hospital to have some fluid removed so he would be more comfortable. I thought this would be an easy procedure, but when the test results came back, his numbers were too high for them to safely extract the fluid. He had been spitting up all day. It was a day I wouldn't want anyone to go through; thankfully, John stayed with me the entire time. He also suggested that the doctors might want to keep Earnie overnight. John told me he could carry Earnie back up the stairs to our house if that is what I wanted to do—so supportive, yet giving me the right to make my decision. This discussion prepared me for what Dr. King suggested, and that was to keep Earnie overnight and make him more comfortable, and if things went better, to do the procedure in the morning. Earnie then told me, "I just can't open the gate." I replied, "Oh honey, put down the buckets; your work is all over with."

I then told Dr. King that we had planned to have Earnie anointed that night at our house, so Dr. King simply suggested that we do it at the hospital. He said he could reserve the solarium for us, and they could wheel Earnie down there. We started to make the calls and tell everyone that instead of coming to our house, to come up to Unity Hospital. The hospital staff brought up coffee and cookies—so thoughtful.

So up everyone came. Father Jim Cassidy had us all participate in the anointing of Earnie, with his grandchildren and their parents gathered around his bed. Fred and Anna, Julie, Rosie, and Father Jim DeBruycker came to support us all. It is not the words I remember that helped me so much, but rather the fact that I saw these faces there to support us. We never have to worry about not being able to have the right words to say to someone; the fact that they know we are there for them is more than enough.

That evening, as we were all getting ready to go home for the night, Montgomery said, "I am going to stay with Grandpa tonight." So I kissed them both goodnight and said, "I'll see you in the morning." The hospital had my cell number if anything came up, but I had put it in the kitchen to charge it, so I never heard their calls. Soon after I woke, just after 5:00 a.m., Montgomery called me to say Grandpa had passed. I told Montgomery I was so grateful he had the last watch.

Then our whole family came up to the hospital, except for the two little girls. We told stories, cried, laughed, and said prayers. That is when I told them about how when I had asked for help for *us,* I got nothing, but when I asked for help for *me,* I got it immediately. I thought maybe they needed to know that for themselves. We stayed for a couple of hours. It was most healing. (Another thing that has been so helpful to me is going to a grief group.)

Later that day, Montgomery and I talked about how he felt having been alone with Grandpa when he died. I asked him, "Was it scary for you?" He replied it was, but he was glad to have been with him. He is nineteen years old and already has been in the room with someone who died whom he loved so much.

On top of Earnie's favorite Irish sweater that he wore continuously, Montgomery had put this letter to me. I didn't find it for a day or two, but it is of course such a treasure to me now, and I wish to share it with you.

His oldest grandson, Montgomery (Monte), had the final watch and this is what he wrote to me.

1/11/11

Grandmother,

I just wanted to start off by saying, I love you! So much. Whenever you find this, tonight, tomorrow, or next week . . . just know I am thinking about you and know that if you ever need to talk, I am here for you.

Last night before the final bag of plasma was started, I was sitting next to Grandpa's bed. I was holding his hand and I said to him, "I do not care if it's your last night in the hospital or your first of one hundred nights here, I will be here for you, 'cause I love you." Right after, I got a good squeeze from his right hand, thumb to pinky squeezing back at my hand. I knew he heard me and understood. I know he will always be with me, just like he will always be with you, forever in our hearts and forever watching over us.

I love you,
Montgomery

We reap what we sow, so let's make sure we are sowing kindness, thoughtfulness, and above all, love in this world! It is our choice.

I think Earnie would end this book with a question and it would be something like this: "So what do you think you are called to do in this world?" Earnie felt we are all called to do something, and no one person's calling is any more important than another's. So what is next for you?

The following is a reproduction of the prayer card from Earnie's memorial program.

In Loving Memory of
Earnie Larsen
Aug. 9, 1939 – Jan. 11, 2011

Mass of Christian Burial at
St. Joan of Arc Catholic Church

Memorial Service at
1st Community Recovery Church

God, grant me the serenity
to accept the things I cannot change,
courage to change the things I can,
and wisdom to know the difference.

Living one day at a time;
Enjoying one moment at a time;
Accepting hardships as the pathway to peace;

Taking, as He did, this sinful world
as it is, not as I would have it;

Trusting that He will make all things right
if I surrender to His Will;
That I may be reasonably happy in this life
and supremely happy with Him
Forever in the next.
Amen.

A visitation was held at St. Joan of Arc Catholic Church on Friday, January 14, 2011.
The Mass of Christian Burial at St. Joan of Arc Catholic Church was held on Saturday,
January 15, 2011. The Celebration/Memorial Service at First Community Recovery
Church was held on Sunday, January 16, 2011.

author biography

Earnie Larsen was a nationally known author and lecturer. He was also a pioneer in the field of recovery from addictive and unwanted behaviors, and the originator of the process known as Stage II recovery. Stage I recovery focuses on breaking a primary addiction or unwanted behavior. Stage I is a release from that destructive behavior. Upon achieving that release, however, the patterns and habits still remain; these feelings and attachments to old systems must be dealt with if recovery is to continue. Resolving these life issues is what makes up Stage II recovery. Earnie also created the Life Management Program, which involves a small-group setting in which the participant works on identifying the negative self-defeating behavior, learns to turn that behavior into a positive one, and has accountability around it.

Earnie authored more than sixty books and forty motivational self-help tapes on a variety of topics ranging from managing interpersonal relationships to spirituality.

As a lecturer, Earnie was known and sought after by businesses, treatment centers, churches, and many other types of organizations, both national and international.

Earnie was seen and heard on television and radio throughout the country, from New York to California to *The Oprah Winfrey Show* in Chicago and interviews on CNN. He is widely read and listened to, and often quoted in Twelve Step groups such as Alcoholics Anonymous, Al-Anon, and Adult Children of Alcoholics. Earnie has been referred to as an authority in dealing with issues such as codependency and dysfunctional behaviors.

Earnie received a master of religious education from Loyola University in Chicago and a degree in counseling with accreditation in chemical dependency and family counseling from the University of Minnesota. Earnie had been a counselor for more than forty years.

Earnie has been called "a big and gentle man with an astounding ability to touch the hearts of those of us who have accepted the challenge of creating change in our lives." But mainly he was a "Gentle Warrior" who helped others with love and a kind heart. He always felt that love was the bottom line. His seminars were frequently sold out, due in part to his unique simplicity and his "heart of America" folksy appeal.

Timeline and Accomplishments

1939
- Born and raised in Omaha

1962
- Received B.A. in philosophy from Immaculate Conception College in Oconomowoc, WI

1965
- Ordained as a Roman Catholic priest in the Redemptorist Order

1966
- Received B.A. in divinity from Immaculate Conception College in Oconomowoc, WI

1966–1970
- Taught religion to African American and Hispanic children in St. Louis, MO

1968
- Wrote his first book, *Good Old Plastic Jesus*, which sold 250,000 copies
- Began his speaking career
- Earnie did extensive counseling and became involved with AA and Al-Anon for the first time

1973
- Received master of religious education from Loyola University in Chicago

1976

- Due to exhaustion, stayed in psychiatric ward at North Memorial Medical Center in Minneapolis, MN, which gave Earnie personal experience with treatment and recovery

1977

- Resigned from the priesthood
- Received a degree in counseling with accreditation in chemical dependency and family counseling from the University of Minnesota
- Joined the ministerial staff at Mercy Hospital in Coon Rapids, MN

1978 to Present

- Began doing seminars and recording audiotapes. Earnie spoke to crowds of between fifty and seventy-five people, then between two hundred and two thousand per evening, including many repeat performances.

- In **1979,** Earnie married. His wife, Paula, currently runs their business and usually traveled with Earnie to his speaking engagements.

- Earnie was heard on hundreds of radio stations and appeared on CNN, *The Oprah Winfrey Show,* and *The Sally Jessy Raphael Show.*

- In **1985,** Earnie began making video series for treatment centers. His first series was on Stage II recovery and consisted of four videos. These tapes were and are used in place of lectures, with discussion questions at the end of each one. Earnie now has more than twenty-four videos for use in treatment centers, prisons, hospitals, halfway houses, and so on. These tapes followed on the heels of his books *Stage II Recovery* and *Stage II Relationships.*

- In **1987,** Earnie created and wrote the initial structure and content of the Life Management Program. Hundreds of professionals have been trained to provide Life Management in the United States, and the program is now also being operated in Australia, England, and Ireland. A later partnership in the early 1990s with Reverend Paul Brunsberg led to the Life Management Office, and with the help of a Bush Foundation grant, Earnie and Paula trained two hundred counselors from Minnesota, North Dakota, and South Dakota to run Life Management groups and work with impaired physicians and lawyers. Also, Earnie and his sister, Carol Larsen Hegarty, through Hazelden published *Days of Healing, Days of Joy.*

- In **1991,** Earnie became a grandfather, which was a life-changing event for him. This same year saw the release of the meditation book *Believing in Myself,* authored by Earnie and his sister, Carol.

- In **1993,** he added a set of four more videos, focusing this time on prisons. Thus began much more involvement with inmates and parolees. Just before this project, he released his book *From Anger to Forgiveness.*

- In **1999,** Earnie partnered with Hazelden to create a four-session curriculum called *Beyond Anger: Connecting with Self and Others,* plus the twelve-session curriculum *From the Inside Out: Taking Personal Responsibility for the Relationships in Your Life.* Both were part of the Life Skills Series for Inmates and Parolees.

- In **2000,** he did a video series on domestic violence, featuring testimonials from victims of abuse. The series both challenges and encourages the abuser to pursue this course of recovery.

- In **2001,** Earnie and Hazelden continued their commitment to inmates and parolees with the criminal justice curriculum *Abused Boys, Wounded Men.*

- As of **2004,** Earnie had written more than sixty books and produced thirty-five videos, fifteen audiotape albums, and more than twenty single audiotapes. The follow-up to his groundbreaking Stage II Recovery books was called *Destination Joy,* released in the fall of 2003. It provides a philosophy of recovery that begins with the recovering person understanding themselves not as an addict first, but as a human being.

- Earnie's book *The Healer's Way,* co-authored with his sister Carol, brings a hands-on compassion to a love-starved world. This powerful, seven-step healing process is drawn from Earnie's thirty years as a pioneering addiction recovery counselor as well as from his personal healing journey.

- Up until he passed, Earnie of course continued to write and speak, but he also considered his volunteering at the Salvation Army and the Union Gospel Mission in Minneapolis and St. Paul an important part of his life's mission. He did a weekly class down at the Salvation Army and sponsored many men. After he was diagnosed with Stage IV pancreatic cancer, he started to write these letters and lessons.

For more information, please visit his newest website: www.changeisachoice.com. His memorial DVD is also on this website.

photos

Earnie's 70th birthday party, August 9, 2009

Erin, Earnie, Paula, and Cara in Earnie and Paula's backyard

See round 8, page 58.

Josh with Earnie two years ago

Josh with Earnie on December 25, 2010

Jan, Earnie, and Paula at a sing-along at the CRC November 2010. This was the last time he was able to attend his dear Wednesday night meeting.

Cara, Paula, and Erin

Earnie and Paula at St. Kate's for the President's Forum Dinner on Friday, May 6, 1994. He didn't dress up like this except on rare occasions.

December 26, 2010—Paula's birthday and two weeks before Second Sunday at Hazelden. He passed one and a half days after Second Sunday.

Earnie, Montgomery, Josh, Ella, Loren, Adeline, Isabel, and Paula at Earnie's 70th birthday

HAZELDEN. BookAid PROGRAM

Each year, Hazelden Publishing reaches out to more than 200,000 underserved people through the Hazelden BookAid Program, providing recovery resources to individuals and agencies in need.

BookAid receives requests for free resources from chemical dependency programs, educational institutions, churches, non-profits, and other organizations from as far away as Uganda, India, and Tibet, and as close to home as our own local county government.

BookAid is run entirely by volunteers and depends upon donations from businesses, Hazelden alumni and staff, and our customers.

Earnie Larsen was a strong advocate of BookAid, and used the program to help those in need for twenty-five years. By doing so, he changed the lives of thousands of people in recovery. If you're interested in carrying on Earnie Larsen's mission by donating to BookAid, please call 888-535-9485 or send a check made out to Hazelden BookAid to the following address:

> Hazelden BookAid Treasury Services
> RW7 P.O. Box 11
> Center City, MN 55012-0011

Hazelden, a national nonprofit organization founded in 1949, helps people reclaim their lives from the disease of addiction. Built on decades of knowledge and experience, Hazelden offers a comprehensive approach to addiction that addresses the full range of patient, family, and professional needs, including treatment and continuing care for youth and adults, research, higher learning, public education and advocacy, and publishing.

A life of recovery is lived "one day at a time." Hazelden publications, both educational and inspirational, support and strengthen lifelong recovery. In 1954, Hazelden published *Twenty-Four Hours a Day,* the first daily meditation book for recovering alcoholics, and Hazelden continues to publish works to inspire and guide individuals in treatment and recovery, and their loved ones. Professionals who work to prevent and treat addiction also turn to Hazelden for evidence-based curricula, informational materials, and videos for use in schools, treatment programs, and correctional programs.

Through published works, Hazelden extends the reach of hope, encouragement, help, and support to individuals, families, and communities affected by addiction and related issues.

For questions about Hazelden publications,
please call **800-328-9000**
or visit us online at **hazelden.org/bookstore.**